A GRAND PARADE

MEMORIES OF CORK CITY LIBRARIES
1855-2005

Edited by
Liam Ronayne

Written by
John Mullins and Liam Ronayne

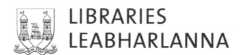

LIBRARIES
LEABHARLANNA

CORK CITY COUNCIL | COMHAIRLE CATHRACH CHORCAÍ

2005

First published in 2005 by Cork City Libraries, 57-61 Grand Parade, Cork, Ireland

ISBN: 0954984708 22

Edited by
Liam Ronayne

Written by
John Mullins and Liam Ronayne

With contributions from
Peggy Barrett, Kieran Burke, Mary Corcoran, Gerry Desmond, Sinéad Feely,
Mary FitzGerald, Breda Hassett, Tina Healy, Patricia Looney, Tim O'Mahony

Personal reminiscences of library users:
Mary Ahern, Michael Cotter, Joan Crowley, Michael Davitt, Séamas de Barra, Su Fagan, Frank Kennedy, Cian Leahy,
Mick Leahy, C.J.F. MacCarthy, Jim McKeon, Joseph Mullane, John A. Murphy, Eoin Ó Catháin, Séamus Ó Coigligh,
Seán Ó Laoi, Eddie O'Connell, Eithne O'Halloran, Noel O'Shaughnessy, Harry O'Shea, Síofra Pierse, Ken Sheffield, Eric Tully
The full text of these reminiscences can be found at www.corkcitylibraries.ie

Graphic design by
Edward Butt

Printed by
City Print, Cork

Contents

Acknowledgements

Without the enthusiastic support of a number of staff and friends of the Libraries this book would not have been possible. Late in 2004 a group of resourceful members of staff came together to prepare a history of Cork City Libraries, using John Mullins' thesis as the basis for the story. Members of the public were invited to write their reminiscences at the same time as the writing of the core text began. This group also assembled the photographs from a wide variety of sources.

Special thanks to

• **Kieran Burke**, for his unique knowledge and insights into all aspects of the city's history, and for his piece on Local Studies.

• **Paul O'Regan** for digitization assistance and all-round electronic wizardry.

• The other staff who wrote pieces on what it is like to work in individual Libraries and departments: **Tina Healy** and **Tim O'Mahony** on the Reference Library, **Mary FitzGerald** on the Rory Gallagher Music Library, **Mary Corcoran** on Hollyhill, **Gerry Desmond** on St Mary's Road, **Sinéad Feely** on Mayfield, **Peggy Barrett** on Douglas, and **Breda Hassett** and **Patricia Looney** on Tory Top.

• **Professor John A. Murphy** for his essay on the Library Committee and the library service.

• **Michael Davitt** as an bpíosa próis agus as an dán a chuir sé chugainn cúpla seachtain sular cailleadh é.

• **Thomas McCarthy** for permission to use his poem 'Cataloguing twelve Fenian novels'.

• The many friends of the library and members of the public who contributed memories and comments, much more than we could accommodate in the book.

• The many staff members and ex-staff members who came up with possible titles of the book, in particular **Michael Plaice** and **Chérie O'Sullivan**.

• **Alun Bevan** of An Chomhairle Leabharlanna for his assistance in sourcing illustrations.

• **Edward Butt**, who was always a pleasure to work with in the design and layout of the book.

Photographic sources

Thomas Crosbie Holdings, Cork City Libraries, Corporate Affairs in Cork City Council, An Chomhairle Leabharlanna, John Mullins, John Sheehan Photography, Michael O'Leary, RTÉ Stills Library

It was not possible to establish the source of a small number of photographs used in the book.

Introduction

A library is more than a collection of books, and much more than the four walls which house it.

It represents for its users not only knowledge and creativity - in the books, CDs and other materials - but also the hopes and dreams which they invest in the library. Theo Dorgan, poet and cultural activist, has said on more than one occasion that the Central Library on the Grand Parade is the intellectual engine room of the city. The warm feelings which the readers have for Cork City Libraries, as quoted throughout the book, would be reason enough to publish it; in fact we have no shortage of reasons.

A Grand Parade: memories of Cork City Libraries 1855-2005 is published to mark Cork's year as European Capital of Culture and the Libraries' central role in the cultural life of the city. It is also published to mark the 150th anniversary of the Public Libraries (Ireland) Act 1855, the first public library legislation in this country. One hundred years ago, in September 1905, the Carnegie Free Library was opened in Anglesea Street, and 85 years ago, in December 1920, it was destroyed along with its contents in the War of Independence.

Grace Neville and Joachim Fischer in their recent book *As others saw us* argue that "Cork most keenly fits historian Pierre Nora's concept of a lieu de mémoire: a place on the landscape charged with emotional meaning and soaked in memories". If this is true for the city, it is equally true for the city's libraries - both the Central Library and the five local libraries. The personal reminiscences which we include bear this out.

This is not a definitive, and certainly not an official, history of the library service but a portrait in words and pictures of how the service has evolved as the city has evolved. As the Lord Mayor says in her preface, it is "an impressionistic account of the library service, flavoured with the insights and memories of some of the countless people who have used and enjoyed the library over decades". Human contact between staff and library users is central to what libraries are and what they do, and we must, in the future, maintain a balance between online services and keeping libraries as a community space with mutually enriching human contact. For the staff, Cork City Libraries represent an extended family. Staff share the anticipation and excitement of book launches, exhibition openings, author visits, opening of new libraries, etc, and are also there to support each other when needed.

150 years after the first public library legislation, 100 years after the opening of the first purpose-built library, and in this once-in-a-lifetime year for the city, it is right both to look back, and to ask what is in store for libraries. Libraries are now concerned with the learning society, with social inclusion, and with a more participative cultural life. For children, libraries offer the first chance and the best chance to open wide the doors to the world of knowledge. Thus Cork City Council sees libraries primarily in terms of resources for the people of the city rather than as buildings or institutions. If Irish society really believes that all citizens have the right of equal access to knowledge, to creative expression, and to the recorded and material heritage, then this right can best be realised through public libraries that have a clear idea of their purpose and are properly resourced.

THE STORY BEGINS

A Grand Parade

Like many cities and towns in the then United Kingdom of Great Britain and Ireland, Cork's first purpose-built public library was funded by benefactor Andrew Carnegie. It is a matter of some irony that, at the high point of the Celtic twilight and Gaelic literary revival, Cork had to look to a Scottish-born industrialist who made his fortune in the United States for its library building. The opening of the Carnegie Free Library on Anglesea Street on 12 September 1905 inaugurated a new phase in the city's library, but it was not, however, the beginning. The story of Cork City Libraries begins not with fanfares and the gala opening but much more modestly, a modesty that Irish public libraries have never lost.

Cork was the first Irish city to adopt the Public Libraries (Ireland) Act, 1855, but it was not until February 1892 that the City Council established a committee to advise on the provision of a public library service. From this committee, with no fewer than thirty-seven members, a committee of management was formed. The latter committee selected the first City Librarian, James Wilkinson, who was appointed in the following October. It appears that a Mr Harrison was first appointed to the job but he sent in his resignation after 13 days. Wilkinson had a remarkable career; born in England he took up the post of City Librarian when Victoria was still on the throne, saw the Library in Cork through

Carnegie Library, Anglesea Street

the Boer War, World War I, the War of Independence and Civil War, and saw his Carnegie library destroyed by his own countrymen. Showing great resilience in the face of adversity, at a time when the new state and the economically depressed city had other priorities, he oversaw the opening of a temporary library in Tuckey Street, spearheaded the building of the purpose-built library on Grand Parade, and remained in the job until 1933, when Eamon de Valera had taken over as President of the Executive Council. He was City Librarian during 41 years which shaped modern Ireland.

In December 1892, within two months of his appointment, Wilkinson opened a public reading room in the Crawford Municipal Buildings, Emmet Place (then called Nelson Place). These buildings included the former premises of the Royal Cork Institution, which were donated to the Corporation along with the Institute's stock of books that later formed the nucleus of the new public library. The reading room was very popular from the beginning, receiving an average of nearly five hundred visitors daily throughout its first year. In July 1893, lending and reference (book) services were inaugurated, proving so popular that the first committee report stated that its 'greatest difficulty is the inability to provide books in sufficient numbers to meet the demands of borrowers'. In the same month this library also provided the first collection of children's books in any Irish public library service.

James Wilkinson

Crawford building, Emmet Place

Carnegie Library, Anglesea Street (© *RTE Stills Library*)

In 1905, the Library service moved from its cramped conditions in Emmet Place to the new elegant building in Anglesea Street designed by architect Henry A. Cutler who was then City Surveyor in Cork. This library, although funded by Carnegie, was built on a site provided by Cork Corporation, incidentally the site now being developed in 2005 for the civic offices adjoining City Hall. The Carnegie Free Library continued the city's pioneering library service to children, this time by providing a separate children's department, which included seating accommodation for thirty children.

Sylvester O'Sullivan, a local journalist, described the Carnegie Library as follows:

"Designed in the Elizabethan or Tudor style, it presented a handsome appearance with its mullioned and transomed windows, its gables and gablets, its entrance loggia and its miniature tower and dome. It was

THE CARNEGIE LIBRARY, CORK, DESTROYED BY FIRE DECEMBER 11-12, 1920

Burned-out shell of Carnegie Library

On a day in May 1919, I made my way from my home on the west of Angelsea Street, across to the Carnegie Library on the east side, where now stands the main entrance to Cork City Hall.

I saw the burning of the Library by Crown forces in 1920, which the public felt to be a blow against them. I was distraught, as if a golden door had been closed against me forever.

C.J.F. MacCarthy

surrounded by a low wall surmounted by ornamental iron railings. The front position of the new library rose to two storeys and the back to one storey. The front was a pretty one, to which the beautiful entrance, balcony, and tower lent attractive effects. The main entrance was in Anglesea Street, a loggia or vestibule opening onto a large open hall. Italian workmen had been especially imported to lay the terrazzo floor. Behind the hall was the central portion of the library, the lending department, and this was flanked on either side by the newsroom and the reference library. Also on the ground floor were the ladies' reading-room and the administrative offices, while overhead were the juvenile library and reading-room. The library had its own heating and ventilation system, a motor-driven fan which circulated through ducts hot or cool air, as the season demanded, through all parts of the building."

Only fifteen years later, however, during the War of Independence, the building, along with many other city-centre buildings, was destroyed by arson attacks started during curfew hours on the night of 11 December 1920 by British military and police. Eyewitness accounts suggest that the destruction of the Library was not a deliberate act; the Crown forces set the City Hall next door alight and the flames spread to the Library. Whether deliberate or not, the Library lost its complete reference bookstock and all lending stock not borrowed at the time, and left Wilkinson with a daunting challenge, but one he was equal to.

After the burning of the Anglesea Street library, the city was without a public lending library for almost four years, until a lending service was restored in temporary premises in Tuckey Street at the end of September 1924.

The building, at No. 2 Tuckey Street, was a Royal Irish Constabulary barracks until it was attacked and burned in June 1921 during the Anglo-Irish war. After the burning of the Carnegie library in Anglesea Street, the Corporation decided in 1923 to refurbish this former RIC building to provide temporary library services. The library in Tuckey Street issued books between June 1924 and May 1930. Playwright Lennox Robinson donated £1,000 towards the cost of equipment in that library. The building now houses offices of the Society of St Vincent de Paul.

Ten years after the burning of the Carnegie Library, a new purpose-built library was opened to the public on a large site, fronted by nos. 57-8 Grand Parade, in September 1930, providing 345 square metres of public floor space, as well as staff quarters, and residential quarters for the City Librarian. The Library was built mainly on the site of former warehouses between Tuckey Street and Kift's Lane. To this day this space forms the nucleus of the Central Library.

Former Library premises in Tuckey Street

1930 facade of 57-58 Grand Parade

Before 'public' libraries

In medieval times, Ireland was renowned throughout Europe for its contribution to learning, and for the libraries which grew up in the monastic centres of learning. These libraries were dispersed after the dissolution of monasteries during the Reformation, leaving Ireland without libraries for over a century, with the exception of those in the hands of a small number of institutions such as Trinity College and a few private individuals.

St Fin Barre's Diocesan Library

The roots of public libraries in Ireland can be traced to the eighteenth century, when Marsh's Library was opened in Dublin as Ireland's first truly public library, and when learned societies established libraries in Dublin, Belfast, Cork, Limerick and Kilkenny. The establishment of the national schools system in the 1830s increased literacy levels, which, in turn, stimulated a desire for post-school learning.

During the 1800s, libraries were re-established by cathedrals, by Mechanics' Institutes, and by membership subscriptions. Some of these libraries, such as that of the Royal Cork Institution, later formed the nuclei of libraries set up on foot of the Public Libraries Acts. From the 1840s, Thomas Davis and other writers in *The Nation* newspaper encouraged readers and the Repeal Association to establish libraries throughout Ireland. After the first of these Repeal Association reading rooms was opened in 1842, many parishes in Ireland established reading rooms to promote a knowledge of Irish culture, literature and history. These reading rooms formed a basis for the subsequent development of statutory municipal and county libraries. By the end of the nineteenth century, the development of library services reflected this widespread desire for people to improve themselves by reading.

In Cork, private institutions provided limited library services before Cork Corporation inaugurated a free public library service. The Church of Ireland Diocesan Library (pictured above), founded in 1720 at St Fin Barre's Cathedral, had a reading room provided for visitors by 1857, opening four hours weekly. This library, however, consisted mainly of theological works. Around the same time, the Green Coat Hospital, a charitable society and school in the city's north side, provided a limited public library service from books donated by clergy and lay benefactors.

The emergence of a wealthy merchant class was reflected in the growth of cultural institutions, such as the Royal Cork Institution (1803), the Cork Literary and Scientific Society (1820), and the Cork Cuvierian Society (1835). Book shops, some with associated circulating libraries, and drawing-room libraries came into existence.

In 1792, local intellectuals founded the Cork Library Society's subscription library, better known as the Cork Library. Its last premises was at the corner of South Mall and Pembroke Street, now a clothes shop but with the sign and date of foundation still proudly over the door (pictured below). This institution, which was open for five hours daily, six days a week, stocked books on a range of serious topics for the promotion of knowledge. General public access to reading facilities was limited by high subscription rates and restrictive admission conditions. The library survived for almost a century and a half as a middle-class institution, until its bookstock was auctioned in 1941.

The libraries of the Royal Cork Institution (1803) and the Minerva Public Reading Room (1819) also favoured the more socially and educationally advantaged, through prohibitive subscription and default fees, and did not provide a library service for the general population in the modern meaning of 'public' libraries. Even the library of the Cork Mechanics' Institute (1825), set up to provide educational reading material for workingmen and which opened nine hours every weekday, charged for book loans and was seen as a competitor to the societies set up for the middle classes, such as the Royal Cork Institution. The reading stocks of these libraries were confined to more serious topics, such as scientific works, theology, travelogues, belles-lettres, art, history and antiquities. For most of Cork's citizens, reading materials were, in effect, luxury items, until Cork Corporation established its own library service in 1892.

Classical design over doorway of former Cork Library premises in Pembroke Street

Ireland's first library law

The 1849 House of Commons Select Committee on Public Libraries was appointed to find the 'best means of extending the establishment of libraries freely open to the public, especially in large towns in Great Britain and Ireland'. The Select Committee reported that, in contrast to some other European countries, there was only one free public library in Britain (in Manchester) and one in Ireland (Marsh's Library, Dublin). Membership of a number of private libraries was available to the public on subscription, but this was a little like saying that everyone could dine at The Ritz.

When the resultant Bill was presented to Parliament it was not universally welcomed. Some MPs argued that financial support of public libraries would require excessive taxation, and that educating the working population would encourage them through 'unhealthy agitation' to rise above their social standing. Those in favour claimed that public libraries should play a positive role in reducing incentives to crime and thus save the government much money.

The Public Libraries and Museums Act, 1850 became law in England and Wales, and was extended to Ireland in 1853. The first legislation providing for the establishment of public libraries specifically in Ireland was the Public Libraries (Ireland) Act, 1855, which empowered Irish municipal and town councils to provide rate-supported free public libraries in towns with a population greater than 5,000. The Act was amended and extended by subsequent legislation in 1877, 1884 and 1894.

ANNO DECIMO OCTAVO & DECIMO NONO

VICTORIÆ REGINÆ.

****

C A P. XL.

An Act for further promoting the Establishment of free Public Libraries and Museums in *Ireland*.
[26th *June* 1855.]

WHEREAS it is expedient to amend the Act of the Sixteenth and Seventeenth Years of Her present Majesty, Chapter One hundred and one, and to give greater Facilities for the Establishment in *Ireland* of free Public Libraries and Museums or Schools of Science and Art: Be it therefore enacted by the Queen's most Excellent Majesty, by and with the Advice and Consent of the Lords Spiritual and Temporal, and Commons, in this present Parliament assembled, and by the Authority of the same, as follows:

I. The said Act of the Sixteenth and Seventeenth Years of Her present Majesty, Chapter One hundred and one, and Section Ninety-nine of the Towns Improvement Act (*Ireland*), 1854, are hereby repealed; but such Repeal shall not invalidate or affect anything already done in pursuance of either of such Acts; and all public Libraries and Museums established in *Ireland* under either of those Acts shall be considered as having been established under this Act. *16 & 17 Vict. c. 101. and Sec. 99. of 17 & 18 Vict. c. 103. repealed.*

II. In citing this Act for any Purpose whatever it shall be sufficient to use the Expression " The Public Libraries Act (*Ireland*), 1855." *Short Title.*

III. In the Construction and for the Purposes of this Act (if not inconsistent with the Context or Subject Matter) the following Terms shall have the respective Meanings herein-after assigned to them; that is to say, "Town" shall mean and include any City, Borough, Town, or Place in which Commissioners, Trustees, or other Persons have been or shall be elected or appointed under the Act of the Ninth Year *Interpretation of Terms.*

4 Q

Readers Remember

My first memory of Cork City Library goes back over eighty years, when I ventured very timidly into the Library in Tuckey Street. I remember the thrill I got when I first joined. It was great to make so many discoveries — taking my time, devoting it totally to a book.

As a young man, I used to spend every Saturday in the City Library, reading, reading, reading. What discoveries I made! So much of my later development and tastes in literature were grounded in library books. Books have guided me throughout life.

I owe the City Library so much. Even now in my ninetieth year, I depend on foundations based on library books that started me off on interests I developed over all those years. In the City Library, I started the study of languages and literature; I started philosophy; I was introduced to so much history, and to a whole lot of interests that remained part of me across the decades. That is something I can never forget for the Library.

I could praise the City Library for ever because it gave me a basic education — something I did not get in any school. I was thought my lessons in school, but got an education through Library books.

Séamus Ó Coigligh

Carnegie and Irish public libraries

Cork's first purpose-built public library was funded by Andrew Carnegie (see picture opposite). As a mark of their appreciation, the city fathers honoured him with the Freedom of the City on 21 October 1903 when he came to lay the library foundation stone. Time was money for Carnegie; he laid the foundation stones for three library buildings — in Waterford, Limerick and Cork — on three consecutive days, 19, 20 and 21 October 1903, and received the Freedom of the City in each.

Who was Andrew Carnegie and why did he fund Irish libraries? Carnegie was born in Dunfermline in Scotland in November 1835 and moved to Pennsylvania when he was 13 as the family followed millions of others seeking a better life through emigration. He made his fortune in steel production in the United States, his business methods being not without controversy, but devoted the latter decades of his life to spending the money for the betterment of society. He inherited a regard for public libraries from his father and uncle who were both involved with the Chartist movement in Scotland. As well as being remembered as a great library benefactor, his name will always be linked with the famous Carnegie Hall in New York which he funded. The percentage of his fortune which came to Irish libraries was small, but it was vital.

In the first half of the twentieth century, Carnegie's money was the most important source for financing new Irish public libraries. The money came originally from Andrew Carnegie himself, and after 1913 from the Carnegie United Kingdom Trust which he set up. As the penny rate allowed in the Public Libraries Acts was too small for local authority financing of new library buildings, the Carnegie grants played a major role in developing the Irish public library service. The Carnegie trust approved applications for funds when they were satisfied that:

- The relevant council had adopted the Public Libraries Acts.
- The relevant council had struck the rate of one penny in the pound for library maintenance purposes.
- A free site would be provided.
- The design of the building was satisfactory.

The scheme was not without its problems. The Carnegie trust responded to applications rather than actively promoting library building, thus the needs of the wider population were not met in a systematic way. As a result, Ireland's sixty-six Carnegie libraries were located in just eleven of the thirty-two counties. In 1927, grants for book purchases were added to the grant scheme for buildings, and by 1950 most public libraries in Ireland had benefited from Carnegie grants.

Andrew Carnegie laid the foundation stone for the Carnegie Library in Anglesea Street, Cork, on 21 October 1903.
The above photograph was taken two days earlier when he was laying the foundation stone for the Carnegie Library in Waterford city.

Library Association conference

The Library Association of Ireland held its first annual conference of 'librarians and others engaged or interested in public library work in Ireland' in University College, Cork from 3 to 5 June 1933.

One delegate, Miss M.K. MacNevin later commented in her impressions of the Cork Conference:

"We were all very sorry when the time arrived to bid adieu to the southern Capital which had bewitched us all by its sociability and beauty during the Whit week-end, and we can only hope that in the not very distant future the call of Cork will be felt so strongly by the librarians that they will have another conference there, although I have a conviction that no conference can be as interesting as our first one has been."

An Leabharlann, Vol. 3(3) September 1933, p.68

The Association's annual conference revisited the City in 1947, 1955, 1985 and 1993.

Delegates at the 1933 conference included the President of the LAI,
Dr. J.F.W. Howley (front row, centre) and ex-Cork County Librarian, Michael O'Donovan,
better known as Frank O'Connor (3rd row, centre).

Decades of calm

Eugene Carberry
City Librarian
June 1933 - May 1955

Dermot Foley
City Librarian
July 1955 - May 1960

James Gaffney
City Librarian
January 1961 - August 1965

The beaten path of my youth was over to St Mary's Road, down Shandona over the North Gate Bridge through the Coal Quay and down the Parade to the City of Cork public library. I have a clear picture in my mind of Eugene Carberry, Librarian, a silver haired, handsome, kindly man, impeccably dressed in grey with silver locks to match. The very personification of what a city librarian should be. I must have traipsed this trip two or three times a week, hail, rain or snow to plunder the treasure trove of Richmal Crompton, Gunby Hadath, WRH Goodyear, not to mention Captain WE (Biggles) Johns . . .

Niall Tóibín*

* *Irish Examiner* 'Property' supplement, 5 Feb. 2005

The years between the opening of the library on Grand Parade and the beginning of the period of major expansion in the early 1970s were ones when little appeared to be happening; the library was content to consolidate itself in the daily life of the city. It was also the time which saw a comparatively rapid turnover of chief librarians, a fact which may not be unconnected to the paucity of development.

Between the retirement of James Wilkinson in 1933 and the coming of Seán Bohan in 1965, the library service was headed by three city librarians, as many as in the remaining 80 years of the library to 2004. Eugene Carberry was the longest-serving of these three, from 1933 to 1955. He was followed by Dermot Foley, one of Irish librarianship's most colourful characters. Having served as City Librarian from 1955 to 1960 he moved to Dublin to become Director of An Chomhairle Leabharlanna / The Library Council. He was followed by James Gaffney, who had the shortest tenure of the city librarians to date, from 1961 to 1965.

In this period the library, through its one and only service point on Grand Parade, provided a service which is still warmly remembered, as evidenced by accounts in this book from borrowers of that era. In a time of few other recreational opportunities, borrowing was high; it was not unknown, especially on a Saturday, to see queues of children out the door of the department and around the corner into the central aisle. On the opposite side of the central aisle there would be a queue of adults heading for the main lending desk. It was a very traditional type of library, as the following photos show.

For the staff of the time it was to a large extent a 'lending factory', as time simply did not allow for the kinds of activities which now characterise a library.

Old Lending department, 1945

Adult Lending check-in desk, 1945

Boy browsing in former Children's department, 1965

Children's department, 1945

Woman browsing in Lending department, 1965

Librarian James Gaffney examining old files of newspapers, 1965

Former newspaper reading room in 1945

Woman reading newspaper, 1965

Men reading newspapers, 1965

An tóstal

—◇—

is invited to the Official Opening by
Prof. Daniel Corkery
of
EXHIBITION OF CORK PRINTED BOOKS,
MSS. ETC.
at
Cork City Public Library,
Grand Parade,
on Tuesday 7th. April, 1953
at 3 pm.

Prof. Daniel Corkery speaking at exhibition of manuscripts and Cork-printed books in Central Library during An Tóstal celebrations in 1953

Display sign from 1947 annual conference of the Library Association of Ireland in Cork

Prof. John A Murphy

Memories of the Library Committee

The development of the Library was greatly assisted over the years by the members of a succession of Library Committees. One of the most noteworthy members was Prof. John A. Murphy, who here remembers his time on the Committee

I served for some years in the 1960s and 1970s as editor of the *Journal of the Cork Historical and Archaeological Society* (JCHAS), and it was in that capacity I was appointed to membership of the Cork City Libraries Committee. The Chairman at that time was the cultured, affable and esteemed Anthony Barry, one time Lord Mayor, deputy and senator as well as, of course, leading tea merchant.

I began my Library Committee membership term in 1966, the year in which Frank O'Connor, the former Cork County Librarian, died. His bust is in the City Library lobby and one can imagine him gazing sardonically at "The Word Endures" exhibition in the spring of 2005, dealing with the malignancy of censorship at different periods in different countries, including our own unfortunate experience. O'Connor, of course, suffered from its petty oppressions, much of his work being banned in the 1940s.

The year after I came on the Committee, Brian Lenihan as Justice Minister began the unbanning process but the censorship mentality was deeply embedded in a prudish and hypocritical society and it lingered for some time among library users. A not inconsiderable amount of our committee time was taken up with po-faced discussions of the "suitability" of certain books which had been submitted by users to us according to the protocol of the marked passage, or indeed the marked individual word. It was a pleasure to have contributed a little to the ending of old foolishness.

At a much later date, I served on the Museum Advisory Committee and had occasion once again to note how cultural services ranked low down in municipal budget priorities. But, to be fair, things have improved, at least in the library's case, in recent years. The inexplicable Monday closures at the Central Library are a thing of the past, as are lunchtime shutdowns. Perhaps as finances improve, we may expect civilised extensions until 10.00 p.m?

The local/newspaper section on the second floor of the Central Library provides and invaluable service for historians and researchers. Schoolchildren are helped with their projects and pursuers of genealogical research are pointed in helpful directions. And you can be sure that, if a local booklet or an issue of JCHAS has disappeared from other collections, you can always depend on the Local section in the Central Library, for the staff will have taken the old-fashioned precaution of keeping the material under lock and key.

Both in branch libraries and in the Central libraries, over several decades I have found the levels of courtesy and efficiency to be always well above the cause of duty. Every user experiences the same diligence and enthusiasm. The staff are a credit to the public service and deserve well of the city.

Prof. John A. Murphy
Emeritus Professor of Irish History,
University College Cork.

Readers Remember

When I was a schoolboy, the library's stock of music books and scores was very small. As this was the only access I had to a range of printed music, I came to know the contents of those few shelves intimately. They served to stimulate my curiosity and feed my imagination until I went to university. I pored excitedly over the scores of the Beethoven symphonies, and came across the names of Bax and Delius.

Most of all I developed an intense longing to hear music which looked so intriguing on the page. There was no record-lending department at that time, until 1978, so it was a question of matching scores and radio broadcasts whenever possible. The subsequent expansion of the Music department is, in my view, the most significant development of the many services provided by the City Library, which now has a widely representative stock of scores and recordings. As a schoolboy who was passionately curious about music, what would I not have given for access to such riches!

Séamas de Barra,
Lecturer, Cork School of Music

Readers Remember

For me the greatest addition to the Library occurred in July 1978, when what was known at that time as the Record Library opened. It began with a few classical and Irish traditional records.

Over the years, that music collection has become one of the largest in the country. As the collection increased over the years, I had the pleasure of listening to music I would otherwise never have heard. I cannot imagine now how someone could live without having heard the beauty of Beethoven, the majesty of Wagner, or the genius of Duke Ellington.

In 2004 I was invited to the formal opening of the Rory Gallagher Music Library. As a lifelong fan and admirer of Rory and his music I felt very privileged to be at the unveiling of one of the most deserved honours that this city has bestowed on one of its sons.

Mick Leahy

The city expands,
the library expands

For its first eight decades, the City Library service operated from just one single city-centre location at any given time. In December 1972, exactly eighty years after the opening of the reading room in Nelson Place / Emmet Place, a branch library was opened in St Mary's Road, facing the North Cathedral on the north side of the city. This was the first local library to open after the city authorities decided to develop a network of library service points throughout the city, following the extension of the city boundary in 1965 which increased the city's population from 70,000 to 125,000. A second branch library was opened a year and a half later on the south side of the city, followed by three more suburban libraries and a mobile library service.

All of these developments took place under the direction of Seán Bohan. Seán, born near Templemore, Co. Tipperary, had served as County Librarian in both Donegal and Galway before taking up the post in Cork. The story of Cork hurling in the late 1950s and early 1960s is a sorry one, beaten virtually every year by Tipperary. By way of compensation, however, the Premier county gave Cork a man who was to build up one of the finest library services in the country. Dr Cornelius Lucey, the high profile RC Bishop of Cork & Ross of that time, prided himself on creating a network or rather a 'rosary' of churches around the city; while one might not normally speak of Bishop Lucey and Seán Bohan in the one breath, the latter left behind him a network of libraries serving the communities of both northside and southside, one which future generations could build on.

St Mary's Road Library

Seán Bohan

42

Former Tory Top Library

Mobile Library, 1975

The city's second branch library opened in July 1974. Tory Top Library served the heart of the southside, from a prime corner site at the junction of Lower Friar's Walk and Tory Top Road. The 1970s building proved unsatisfactory and was replaced by a new library on this site, which opened in 2005. In October 1975, a Mobile library service was launched, providing day-long services to six areas of the city each week. This mobile library served three sites north of the river Lee, at Gurranabraher, Blackpool, and Mayfield; and three on the south side, at Bishopstown, Ballinlough, and in the Blackrock area. In the late 1970s, the mobile library issued more children's books than the central children's library or any one of the branch libraries.

Since then, the Mobile service was gradually cut back to open only two days per week, as three more branch library services were opened in the suburban locations of Douglas (November 1976), Hollyhill (December 1980), and Mayfield (November 1984).

During a three-year period from the mid to the late 1970s the Central Library was redeveloped, with much greater street frontage on the Grand Parade, and much enhanced facilities. For some years it was the largest single public library building in Ireland.

Before & after: Book storage and sorting before opening of extended Central Library in 1978

Before:
Refurbishment of premises at 57-8 Grand Parade

After:
Frontage of Central Library at 57-61 Grand Parade after refurbishment and extension in the late 1970s

The importance of the local libraries is shown by the fact that, when the city's third branch library opened in Douglas in 1976, the combined total of books borrowed each month from the mobile library and three branches was greater than the total borrowed from the Central Library. The total membership in the local libraries also overtook Central Library membership in the same month in 1976. Overall totals for items borrowed across the network rose with the opening of (1) the new and much larger Central Library adults' lending department in August 1977, (2) the new Central children's department, in November 1976, (3) the Central music department, in July 1978, (4) the Hollyhill Library in the north-west suburb of Hollyhill–Knocknaheeny, in December 1980, and (5) the Mayfield Library in the city's north-east, in November 1984.

The Hollyhill Library initially opened in the Terence MacSwiney Community College in 1980, later being transferred to the nearby Hollyhill shopping centre where it is now located. Thus within a twelve-year period from 1972 to '84, five branch libraries and one mobile library were added to the service, and the Central Library premises were redesigned and extended, a wonderful tribute to Seán Bohan's vision and leadership.

Interestingly, the Douglas library, situated in a shopping-centre site straddling the city–county border, is jointly funded by Cork City Council and Cork County Council, while the staffing, stocking, and the day-to-day running of the branch is a matter for Cork City Libraries. The Douglas Library has the highest number of registered members and number of items borrowed among the local libraries in Cork City Libraries' network.

Mayfield Library, officially named Frank O'Connor Library in October 1999

Hollyhill Library: Demonstration of online services

Hollyhill Library external view

Douglas Library external view

Douglas Library: Gramophone Circle meeting

Putting children first

Many members of staff have raised the profile of children's services over the years, including for example Patricia Egan and Margaret Linehan, who served together between 1978 and 1993. During that time the profile of service to children was vastly enhanced through an extraordinary range of activities, attracting very large numbers of young readers, and much media interest both locally and nationally in the process.

A few examples of the initiatives will serve to illustrate this exciting time for children's services.

1991: Pat Egan (left) & Margaret Linehan (right) welcoming the then Rose of Tralee, Denise Murphy, to charity event in Library

Broadcasting
Margaret and Pat presented regular monthly book reviews/discussions on RTÉ Cork Local Radio, and also contributed to radio and television programmes promoting Cork City Libraries. For instance, Pat was interviewed on RTÉ1 about the censorship of Eric Cross's *The Tailor and Ansty* and Margaret featured on RTÉ1 television programmes including *TeleTalk* with presenter Ciana Campbell, and on *Bookside* with presenter Doireann Ní Bhriain, as well as on a number of local television programmes.

Children's book club celebrating its sixth anniversary in 1991

Book Club for children
The story of the book club for 10- to 14-year-olds is told below. Cultural trips for members was a feature of the book clubs. Trips were taken to places of literary interest in London, Belfast, Dublin and around Cork city and county. The children's and adult book clubs used to meet jointly during Children's Book Festivals, when members shared stories, played different music favourites, and exchanged views on everyday concerns.

The 'Story Car'

In the mid 1980s a car was fitted out with loud speakers and music to attract children, leading to summer open-air story readings in suburban housing estates not served by local libraries. This was in addition to train trips to Fota Wildlife Park to read stories to children. During the Cork800 celebrations in 1985, staff organized story-boat trips between Cork and Cobh for a total of 400 passengers, who were entertained by author readings, games, songs, and a book fair, along with many story sessions.

1985: Story Car bringing story time to children in city suburbs

City Library float

Pat and Margaret organized a float for Cork City Libraries in the city's St Patrick's day parade in 1987. The float — designed around the theme of the old woman who lived in a shoe and had so many children she didn't know what to do — advertised the library as the ideal place for all children. Children from each local library participated in the parade, and the float won first prize for originality.

Prizewinning St Patrick's Day float, 1987

National profile

Margaret and Pat were avid readers of children's books and active members of the Youth Libraries Group of the Library Association of Ireland, contributing reviews to its annual reading lists for children. The Children's Book Festival each October was a time in which they worked particularly hard to promote library services for children, attracting increased media coverage and increased visits to children's libraries. Some Book Festival events drew so many children that extra space in the nearby Grand Parade Hotel had to be availed of.

Pat Egan wrote two children's books, *St Patrick and the Snakes* and *St Brigid*, and remained a very active member of society after her retirement in 1993, while Margaret moved on to a career in higher education. The legacy of the synergy between Pat and Margaret, and their exceptional focus on and enthusiasm for promoting and delivering library services to children, helped to establish Cork City Libraries' flourishing children's services.

Book Festival in Grand Parade Hotel, 1989

Children's Book Club, 1985-1993

A discussion with a group of teenagers at Children's Book Festival in October 1984 led to the formation of Ireland's first children's book club in Cork City Libraries in January 1985. Readers from 10 to 14 years of age pointed out that, though they read widely, they had no-one to share and enjoy their reading experiences with, and were often at a loss regarding recommended titles and authors for their age-group.

This was an opportunity for library services to encourage young people to come together to discuss, share and recommend reading choices, and the opportunity was seized. The club was set up with 12 kids initially; it quickly became clear that the formula for the meetings was succeeding and, in response to requests, friends of existing members and other applicants were granted membership.

In March 1989 a second club was formed when the number of members reached thirty. Monthly meetings took place with each member present recommending and synopsizing a book of his or her choice. When other people present had already read the particular book, short discussions about the book took place. Conflicting opinions about the same book often made the meetings even more interesting. Each meeting ended with the co-ordinator of the club recommending about six to eight titles of her choice, suitable for the age profile of club members. Material ranged from new publications to older well-established authors but always across a variety of themes and a wide range of interests.

The book club members were not satisfied with just reading and discussing. Members frequently wrote book reviews published in the *Evening Echo* and elsewhere. A video of Frank O'Connor's short story "My First Confession" was made, with filming and sound-recording by members themselves. The video was entered in the 1986 Junior International Film Festival and won the overall award — a first for an Irish group — as well as winning the awards for best actor and actress. A 'Reading Tree' was introduced as a supplementary incentive to club members and non-members, in the 10 to 14 age group, to read ten specially chosen titles each summer. As readers returned one of these books, they discussed the storyline

RTÉ1 television recording of Children's book-club meeting in 1988

with the children's librarian before being awarded a green leaf-shaped certificate containing the book's title and the reader's name, which was then fixed to the branches of what started as a bare tree in the library. The tree was quickly covered in paper leaves.

The book club also produced a biannual magazine consisting of book reviews, short stories, jokes, cooking recipes, cartoons, etc. designed and produced by book club members. The magazine was sold in the library and proceeds from the magazine were used to supplement book club touring costs. In July 1988 another highlight for club members was the RTÉ1 television recording of some of their book discussions and views on club activities, broadcast on the *Bookside* literary programme — the first time an outside TV broadcasting team visited Cork City Libraries.

During the years of the children's book club, the central children's library saw a buzz of activity throughout the long school holidays each year, motivated by the excitement of informal gatherings with peers and a librarian who shared their passion for reading. Looking back at the club over its eight years, 1985-93, former members and their parents have no doubt that the children's book club had a significant influence on the development of literary, academic, and life skills of club members.

1992: Fiona Murphy, winner of library competition, meeting celebrity chef Darina Allen, with Children's Librarian Margaret Linehan and Fiona's mother Aideen

Readers Remember

A Memory of the Bookclub: the Reading Tree
  The Book Club was a haven of book-gulping kids. Best of all was that magic week early in the summer when the 'reading tree' was launched. Our librarian would provide a long list of brand new books and challenge us to read them all in a few weeks. Many of us read one a day and had our names up on paper leaves on the 'reading tree'.
To have a librarian listen to us, uncritically, to know that she had also read the books — magic! It was so unusual to be taken seriously and it became a very serious task. How proud we were when we had read all those texts and filled the tree with leaves. Then we avidly looked for more. More. More! And that was long before the comfortable uniformity of a Harry Potter. We all have fond memories of those great Book Club days and those long, never-ending bookish summers.
  Dr Síofra Pierse

Club Léitheoireachta na nÓg
Is beag rud ba mhó a spreag chun léitheoireachta mé agus mé óg ná Club Léitheoireachta na nÓg i Leabharlann na Cathrach. Do mhúscail reachtaire an chlub an tsuim agus an grá a bhí aici don léitheoireacht i measc na bpáistí a fhreastail ar na cruinnithe rialta insan Leabharlann. Bhí an-am agam sa chlub léitheoireachta agus is mór an trua nach bhfuil a leithéid ann a thuilleadh.
  Eoin Ó Catháin

Readers Remember

When my favourite librarian, who shall remain nameless, told me that I could renew books over the phone, I was ecstatic and even more so when at a later stage she informed me that I could now use the Internet for this purpose.

The greatest pleasure for me by far was the opening of the Music Library. I have had a lifetime interest in music, but this has been in a small well-defined area. Now it becomes possible to explore, leisurely and in depth, areas with which I was totally unfamiliar.

Dr Eric Tully

Readers Remember

Seventy years ago I met up with a friend in St Peter's & Paul's primary school who lived near the Cork City Library. I lived about 5 minutes walk away from the Library. We joined the Library together; the library had a profound effect on me and changed my life for ever.

Frank Kennedy

A long time ago I was a fledging member of the Cork City Library, having acquired my ticket in the Children's Department, for the sum of one (old) penny.

The acquisition of this penny ticket, which had to be renewed annually, was the beginning of my acquaintance with Cork City Library and was the "Open Sesame" to a treasury of books, literature and the knowledge of the many things that can make life worth living.

Eithne O'Halloran

Cataloguing twelve Fenian novels

THOMAS MCCARTHY

335.04

Dampness has eaten away at the *Dunferry Risin'*.
Ninety years have waterlogged the author's name:
Moran is missing, only *J.J.* survives
in the grey fog of the spine –
the author as his mother knew him
or as the IRB might have known him
in the familial secretive world.
It was praised by an MP in *The Evening Sun*,
generous in Victorian London's neutrality.
This is the best picture ever of the IRB.

398.21

Lennox, should we move you from fiction to 398?
For years you haven't moved from the fiction shelf;
your *A Young Man from the South* is brown with rot,
should we throw it out? The folklore
that coloured your pen was overwhelming
and overwhelmed so many with love –
love of country is such a blessed thing,
Fay's Abbey Theatre, Yeats' *Kathleen Ni Houlihan*.
We've moved from Willie to Enoch Powell,
from the soft porn of Lennox consumed
to the steel horn, hard as Wolverhampton nails.
Lennox, welcome to the sceptical librarian
who hauls you out of time, fiction and pain.

941.591

Rain seeps through the hoarding on the broken window;
Corkery rain, insistent, dramatic.
Youths are playing darts against the library
door, challenging me to respond:
public servant, hated. Bull's eye!
Tina, these two are gone mouldy, will I
throw them out? A note from Sheila
attached to *The Whiteboys* by Mrs S.C. Hall
and D.M. Lenihan's *The Red Spy* –
the red spy a Dublin Castle agent
forever on the threshold of quiet, of death.

364

This is what fiction can do to a country:
a battle-cruiser in the Gulf, destroyers off Blackpool
for the conservative conference. Who will
unwind the paranoia? The poets? The courts,
God help us. There is the question of the Birmingham Six,
Diplock Courts, the literally bloody mess
left by a murdered machine, botched revolution.
Too many brushes with the wrong tribunal –
I commit Canon Sheehan
to the library trash-can,
seven pages missing from his *Glenanaar*
as pages have fallen away from the statute books
to expose the raw powers of the state.
Too late to save *Glenanaar*, its conspirators,
the late Canon's quality of remembrance.
This is what terror can do to a novelist.

920

George Bartram, this can't be your life-story;
Fisher Unwin's *White-Headed Boy*
that has languished in the biography section
for twenty years, another Irish tale
to satiate the post-Pre-Raphaelites.
Bertram, who are your children's children?
Did you know the Sinn Fein candidate,
Louis Walsh – the South Derry hopeful?
– Louis has drawn a pen-portrait of '48,
The Next Time, with O'Connell, Duffy, Davis.
The whole of our lives, a hundred years
of biography masquerading as novels
and novelists moonlighting as MPs.
Ours was an abrupt and botched revolution;
Coitus interruptus, impermanent as binding-wax.

327.415

Power after absolution, chimeric prestige,
prison is the perfect background for an MP
When We Were Boys is what William O'Brien
made of two years inside.
Longmans in the '90s, then Maunsel in '18
bought his Glengariff story.

O distant country!
O broken dreams!
For liberation is a valley of disappointment –
after power, the mere excitement of museums.

630

The past is so rural and intimate, if we forget
the rotted corpse in ditch-water, hooded
and whole streets disembowelled like spineless books.
The past has charm like cut glass or wickerwork:
beware of novelists throwing or weaving that –
Alexander MacArthur's *Irish Rebels* or Lysaght's
Her Majesty's Rebels, their stress of contradictions
like the stress at the apex of heavy thatch.
Their spines have fallen apart, and their stories
withered. Rotted cords, decaying sallie-rods.
They wished to keep two things going at once,
the aesthetic being and the ethnic predicament.
Mr Lysaght, your book is committed to the *worn-out* bin
- like our view of history, from Davis to 1891.

823.BER

The hard cover of this novel comes away in my hand,
the desecrations of time,
like the desecration of farms and great houses
for the common good.
Mr Butler of *The Bad Times* was hauled
into truth, manhandled, as disappointed as Isaac Butt.
For the liberal mind cannot stand violence
as the propertied abhor agrarian unrest –
what is it that we cannot bear to lose?
Binding thread hangs from this damaged book
as corpses hung, feather-like,
from the unpainted gibbet of the nineteenth century.
Our past was in these words, *The Bad Times*
as quiet now as the hanging man without land.

821.LAW

Sweet daughter of our Lord Cloncurry, Emily
Lawless, you wrote *Hurrish* in a hurry in a hurry
and it flourished for you, for years.
What right did you have to make such fiction
out of death? Was your heart with the Land League?
I'd say not:
no more than the true heart of Longfellow
was in the breast of the Red Indian prince.
Now the world is bleak, by café or lake.
I can only think your mutilated book
is a song like Hiawatha's,
so dark we must eat our fear together.

The library now . . .

Patricia Looney reading to children, 1994

Hanna O'Sullivan (left) succeeded Seán Bohan as City Librarian and served until 2003. Hanna, a native of Castleisland, Co. Kerry, had previously been County Librarian in Carlow. During her term, Hollyhill Library moved to much more appropriate premises in the Hollyhill Shopping Centre, but the most important innovation in library services in her term was the adoption of information & communications technologies, described below.

Since the 1990s, public-access computers are very popular

At the beginning of the twenty-first century the library service in Cork has changed radically and yet still follows the same principles. It is as its founders wished it to be: the university of the common man and woman, the arts centre of the common man and woman. The library has changed perhaps as much in the last decade as in the previous 100 years, and especially since the government's *Branching Out* policy.

The library now: learning for all

It is a daily reality in any of the libraries in the city network to see staff helping post-primary and third-level students engaged in course work, adults returning to work and to full-time or part-time study, and other students pursuing formal courses. Library staff support distance learning, for example the Open University, and are increasingly involved in partnerships with state and voluntary bodies in the education sector. Helping people with literacy problems, and helping the 'new Corkonians' in mastering English is also a feature of today's libraries.

Brian Manning IT tutor from National Council for the Blind with student

All library service points have experienced a steady increase in the volume and complexity of information requests. This coincides with changes in the primary and secondary education systems, which require students to engage in project work on their own, and this places a far greater burden on public libraries to collect, index, and search for data to serve these growing demands. The substantial growth in the number of third-level students over the last two decades has led to more demands for information services from library staff, in Central and local libraries. Society in general is putting a greater emphasis on formal and informal lifelong learning, and the almost ubiquitous use of information technology has accelerated this growth. An educated population tends to make more sophisticated demands for higher quality library-information services.

While enquirers use the internet for general enquiries, the expertise of library staff is called on to locate information not so readily available on the internet. New products – CD-ROMs, online products – require training and familiarisation on the part of staff before they can, in turn, help the public make best use of them.

The library now: culture for all
Cork City Libraries' Central and local libraries are uniquely popular and non-commercial public spaces that attract all sectors of society. They are recognised as places without boundaries of class, age, wealth, religion or race;

they are spaces where one may sit, read, browse, visit an exhibition or attend a reading or recital. Whereas some other cultural venues can be formal and intimidating, people see libraries as welcoming and familiar; people who regularly use the library can often be hesitant in attending or participating in arts events.

In a city very proud of its cultural institutions – Opera House, Crawford Gallery, Everyman Palace, etc. – it is worth recording that the library service is still the major facilitator of local cultural expression, not least through its work in promoting literature and reading, and in local studies provision. Libraries are fostering the traditional and contemporary arts; exhibitions of paintings and photographs, poetry readings and author visits, exhibitions and talks on local history, and other arts and heritage events are held in the Central Library and local libraries on a weekly basis. Libraries also support the Gaelic language and enhance its use in the community at large, especially through the Ciorcal Comhrá and Cúpla Focal groups which flourish in Central, Tory Top and Douglas Libraries.

Lucy Stewart reading to children, 2002

1993: Introduction of computer-assisted library circulation systems — (left to right) Fidelma Collins (Library Committee Chair), Lord Mayor Micheál Martin, Seán Kelly (Interleaf Technology), John Mullins (Systems Librarian), Hanna O'Sullivan (City Librarian), and Niall Bradley (Assistant City Manager)

The Library now: computers enter the scene

Cork City Libraries celebrated their centenary in 1992. In that year the Council designated a senior member of staff as systems administrator with responsibility for project-managing the implementation of a computer system to manage library operations: the issuing and return of books and the maintenance of accurate catalogues. With the help of four contract staff, digital catalogue records were soon created for the library's 200,000 older stock of books, journals, and sound recordings. In August 1993, the permanent cataloguing staff also converted to electronic database creation for all newly purchased stock. By mid-1995, the library's 166,000 stock of circulation books had been added to the database, and from that time an acquisition package has been used to support the ordering, purchasing, and acquisition of new books and sound recordings.

In 1993, the Library very appropriately marked one hundred years of lending services when Mayfield library became the first service point in the city network to implement computerised lending of stock. The table below indicates the dates in which automated circulation processes were put into effect in the branch libraries and Central departments.

**DATES OF PHASED IMPLEMENTATION
OF COMPUTER-AIDED CIRCULATION**

Service-point	Date of implementation
Mayfield Library	10 March 1993
Central Children's department	27 April 1993
Central Adults' department	1 February 1995
Tory Top Library	3 October 1995
Hollyhill Library	25 November 1997
St Mary's Rd Library	30 July 1998
Douglas Library	26 August 1998
Music library (sound recordings)	14 May 2002

For the first seven years, computerisation was a joint project between Cork City Libraries and Cork County Library. A single host computer, housed and administered in Cork City Libraries, was shared by the two library services, while network support was administered by Cork County Council. Since 1999, ICT network support for Cork City Libraries is administered by the City Council Information Systems unit.

Greater access to online library-catalogue information offers many advantages to library users, who now enjoy 24-hour online access. During the 1990s, the traditional card catalogue, listing only local branch or department holdings of books, was replaced by public computer catalogue terminals throughout library premises, showing the holdings of all departments and branches. These terminals were phased in when each branch library was linked to the Central Library's host computer. Since October 2001, the catalogue is available on the World Wide Web. As well as searching the catalogue, users may also reserve items and renew borrowed items online. The web-based catalogue, at www.corkcitylibraries.ie, also provides access to a very useful in-house index of selected topics from newspapers, periodicals, and other items in stock. This unique index is very helpful for enquirers researching articles relating to Cork, Ireland, and further afield, as well as general topics on social issues, science, biography, business, and other information.

The crucial importance of ICT for library services is reflected in the steadily increasing number of individual workstations — from an initial 4 in 1992, to 84 at the end of 2000, and 135 (75 for public; 60 for staff) in 2005. Cork City Libraries introduced its first internet workstation in June 1996, as a reference resource. In the following year, internet service was extended by providing one public internet workstation in each of the library premises throughout the city and in each department of Central Library.

Screen capture of online services

Digitization project: (left to right) Ruth Buckley (Head of Information Systems), Joe Kennelly (Director of Services), Liam Ronayne (City Librarian), with digitization team, Kieran Burke, Paul O'Regan and John Mullins

The number of public-access workstations providing internet across the five city branches and Central Library totalled 55 in December 2000, and 75 in September 2005.

The library now: digitization and the world wide web
In autumn 2004, Cork City Libraries initiated a project to create a web site to host digitized material relating to Cork. With grant aid from the Department of the Environment, Heritage, and Local Government's National Digitization Strategy, Cork City Libraries began to develop digitization and related services, and the first digitized images went online in November 2004.

New material is continually added to this site, at www.corkpastandpresent.ie. What was previously available only during library opening hours is now available online, twenty-four hours a day. This not only benefits library users, but also reduces damage to materials from excessive handling, helping to preserve older and more valuable items of stock. The first online images added to the site included historical maps and photographs of the city with accompanying texts, articles from selected journals, and bilingual lists of city street names, rivers, townlands, buildings, and other geographic features.

Local Studies

Local studies, local history. What images do the phrases conjure up to the uninitiated? Dusty tomes and droning old bores half-desiccated with learning? The reality is so different. A posse of children excitedly poring over old newspapers and maps. How do you show them how to handle the materials with care without damaging their enthusiasm? Decisions. Every day.

Genealogical researchers come from all over the world. New Zealand, South Africa, Canada, the U.S.A. They have travelled in hope for thousands of miles. Some of them, alas, with little background knowledge will find little about their families. 'Where was your great grandmother from?' 'Julia O'Sullivan from West Cork'. How do you tell them their chances of finding anything about her are vanishingly small after such an odyssey?

Sport. A stream of people with immense knowledge of their sports spending hours, days, years reading newspapers, lovingly recording the details of the histories of their clubs and their sports. A fond memory. A colleague with no interest in sport was asked for information on the boxer 'Pakie' Mahoney. Consternation on colleague's face. Probably thought Mahoney was a member of an extremist group. I intervened. "Didn't he fight Billy Wells?' Immediate smile on the face of the inquirer. 'Fair play boy, you're one of our own.'

Newspapers. An immense source of information on all aspects of local studies. How to organize it, make it available to people? Index it, stupid! The old card index was laborious to compile with few points of access. 1996 brought computerised indexing with a kaleidoscope of access points. Nirvana.

Local historians. Amateurs. Some of them professional historians but all of them amateurs who love their subjects. All good local histories are labours of love. The people of Cork owe them all, past and present, an immense debt. In sensible countries they would name streets after them.

Local publications. An endless flood. How to keep track of all of them? Constant examination of newspapers and catalogues, visits to bookshops. Still some get through the net. Aggravation.

New colleagues. They seem intimidated at first. Their faces say 'How will I ever master this body of information?'. How do you eat an elephant? One bite at a time. Three months later colleague is answering a difficult query with aplomb. Told you so!

Satisfaction. Oh yes. To help collect the memory of one's own place and people. To help preserve the 'knowledge that's too humble to know it's knowledge', in J.M. Coetzee's marvellous phrase about local customs, songs, games and other seemingly unimportant aspects of local culture. A privilege.

Kieran Burke

Lucy Stewart assisting a group of enquirers in the Local Studies department

Kieran Burke introducing a school class to online local studies services

Reference Department, Central Library

Reference Library

Any day in the Reference Library is about the people of Cork and their information needs. Days are filled with questions from researchers, consumers checking the best buys, DIY devotees, businessmen and do-it-yourself legal eagles. We are frequently asked to find poems from first or other lines, addresses, telephone numbers and the last cryptic crossword clue. People who ask questions often have interesting stories to tell about their lives or events they remember.

"What colour is my aura?"

"Have you a video of the 1798 rising?"

"Can I have a picture of steam rollers in the Middle Ages?" These are some of the unanswerable questions put to the Reference Library staff and are almost the only questions we will not attempt.

The Reference Library is an information and research centre with valuable collections on literature, history and art, current affairs and many other areas. This storehouse of knowledge is stored in newspapers, books and journals. Access to the Internet and other electronic databases enhances the collection and increases our ability to answer questions we are asked.

Our clientele changes with the seasons. From autumn to spring many students of all ages visit for project work, particularly on history and the social sciences. During the school year, class visits from secondary schools and post-leaving-certificate colleges fill our days with new generations being introduced to the wealth of the Reference Library. A queue of students hopeful of a study place can be seen outside the premises in the mornings before the start of the Leaving Certificate examinations.

In summer we welcome foreign students. They come to learn about Irish culture and to tackle information on hurling and Gaelic football with great enthusiasm. The Reference Library is often one of the first places visited both by tourists and new city residents; it is a welcoming and democratic place for all.

The atmosphere in summer is calmer. Our daily visitors who come to read the newspapers welcome the quieter atmosphere during these months. There is a long tradition of newspaper reading-rooms in public libraries.

I sometimes think we are detectives trying to find some elusive fact. At other times we are educators, not in the formal sense, but acting as guides for students finding their way through the available sources. We are collectors, custodians, information specialists.

The Reference Library continues a long tradition of providing information and education for the people of Cork and further afield. Hopefully, it will enhance the knowledge of its users for generations to come.

Tina Healy

Reference Library reminiscences

I worked in the Central Reference Library for ten years in the 1980s. It was a difficult time for libraries: staff were in short supply, book funds and opening hours were cut. It was a time when the philosophy of 'make do' and 'do the best you can in bad circumstances' was the order of the day. But there were good things too. There were no targets, no performance audits, no marketing, no publicity drives. Libraries were still seen as part of a public service which people valued, now they are more of a business venture with all the attendant pressures of that.

Despite all the staff shortages we seemed to have more time to talk to people and engage with our customers. The following cameos may give some idea of those more innocent times. One of the funniest things that happened to me was the 'case of the uncomfortable dog'.
It happened like this:

A man in his thirties came to the desk and told me that his collie had an itch. The first thing that went wrong was that I thought he said 'colleague', the second thing was that I had that morning made up my mind that I would listen for the unspoken question behind the ordinary query – I had been at a library seminar the week before. I brought him down to the medical encyclopedias, my mind furiously working over the various ways one could catch an itch from a colleague, and telling myself I'd manage this very sensitively. The client seemed a bit embarrassed. 'Here are the medical encyclopedias', said I, 'you can work away there if you want and call me if you need anything else'. 'Ah sure, I'd hardly catch it from him at all', said he. 'You couldn't be too sure', said I, in an admonitory tone. 'Sometimes you can be working very close to a colleague, and 'twould all depend on what was causing it, and that.' 'Ah sure, boy,' tisn't a colleague at all,' tis my collie dog has a bit of the mange', said he. 'Oh God', said I, 'I'd want to have my ears examined.' I was beginning to have a very bad fit of the giggles, and I thought the best way out of it was to have them and be finished with it, and hope that the client would see the funny side of it. 'Give me a minute', I said, 'I'll have to take some time out to have a laugh', and there we were, the two of us, in stitches between the shelves. We eventually made our way to the veterinary section, and I suppose your man was saying to himself 'What in the hell is up with that fella, there's one born every day.' But fair play to him, he had his laugh too.

Another day a schoolgirl came up to me on a busy Saturday afternoon. I was on my own, crowds milling around, people looking for yesterday's paper, children doing projects, and whatever. 'Have you anything about the crab nebula?', said she. To be honest I hadn't a clue what she was talking about. 'Tis up in the sky', she explained, but I was doing my best to sidestep the query. She was only a schoolgirl and a bold one at that, I thought, when I felt a fatherly arm on my shoulder. It was the late C. J. F. MacCarthy, at that time the chairman of the Library Committee, and a man with the greatest respect for libraries and learning. 'Remember the first professor of astronomy in Maynooth was a lady', he said with a smile, and walked off. I'd have benefited from a library seminar that week, but at least I now knew that the crab nebula was an astronomical object. Years afterwards I saw that same girl on a television show discussing some very complicated matters, and I thought of my busy Saturday afternoon and my glib answers.

Then there were the visiting characters. I remember the lady in red and the lady in green, and the lady who asked me to keep a bicycle chain in safekeeping for her as it was a family heirloom. I had seen the lady in red sitting on a step in Grattan Hill on the evening before she turned up in the library, after she got off the Dublin train at Kent Station. In the library, she offered to confer the most amazing sexual favours on us free of charge if only we'd listen to whatever messages of doom she had come to proclaim in Cork, but we declined politely. The lady in green took more of a shine to my colleague; she was wrapped in four or five green veils and a huge flowery green hat. We always noticed that the characters would favour either of us (there were only two of us working in the department then), and it was only with a bad grace that they would deal with the one who wasn't their favourite.

We also learned the rudiments of sign language from a regular client who was profoundly deaf, to facilitate communication with him when he wished to request particular newspapers. Some clients would ask us to write letters for them, to fill forms, or enter newspaper or magazine competitions for them. Many were the days when a worried-looking client would come to the desk and say 'I think there's a dead man in the far corner, I'm very worried'. But it would only be a refugee from the newsroom downstairs who wasn't able for the rough and tumble of that institution who would come to read the newspapers in the relative comfort of the Reference Library, and then take off his shoes and fall asleep in the heat. I'd wake up the latter-day Lazarus before closing and he'd toddle off home. Then there was the elderly gentleman who used to kill his fleas by crushing them between the pages of a book, and the three English men who used to bring in a pound of butter and eat it with no accompaniment of bread or biscuit. Eventually one of them rushed up to me and asked me where was the nearest police station. I showed them how to get to the Bridewell, they all ran out and we never saw them again.

My last story will be of the magic-mushroom man. He came to me and asked if we had any books about magic mushrooms. I said I'd have a look and he followed me around. I found a book eventually but no sooner had I put it in his hand than he ran out of the room and I heard afterwards that he took a flying leap over the security barrier with his treasure trove, and was never seen by us again. Those were the days. The clients kept us entertained and no doubt we kept the public entertained, discussing our private lives in loudish whispers in the long quiet room in the long quiet summers of the nineteen-eighties.

Tim O'Mahony

A Day in the life of the Rory Gallagher Music Library

Is there a typical day in the music library? No. Are there typical users? No. They are people who love music, performers and budding performers browsing through scores for that all-important audition piece, or that song from the 50s or 60s to sing at a friend's birthday party or maybe in a talent contest, members of choirs and choral societies, songwriters, composers, students and teachers.

The importance of music to music lovers is confirmed every day, for example by a teacher on returning to work in early September as she eagerly renewed her membership declaring, 'I am back at school only a week and am already stressed: I need music!'

In the music library, we get to know students from the time they start their courses to the time they finish. We see them grappling frantically with last-minute assignments or listening to a piece they are about to play in a practical exam within a few hours.

Finding song words is always interesting. At times the person looking for the song may know only some of the words and the air, and will whistle or hum the air or sing those words. Staff have been known to join in and, in the interaction, we usually identify the song, provide the words, and play or lend a recording.

Impromptu choral sessions also take place from time to time. One morning a lady who was looking for the words and music of 'One Alone' from The Desert Song was serenaded by one of our regular users when he cleared his throat and began 'I have heard all that you have been saying . . .' By the time he got to 'One alone to be my own . . .', three other people had joined in the singing.

I was working in the music library only a short while when a girl asked me for 'two-pack CDs'. Assuming she wanted a double CD, I asked her 'What type of music?' She answered 'Any two-pack CDs'. I started to say we had classical, folk, Irish, but, noticing the look of incredulity on her face, I knew I was on the wrong track. Then, I saw that my young male colleague had moved away from the desk in tears of laughter. I excused myself and walked towards him; they composed themselves just enough to tell me she was looking for Tupac Shakur.

Many a discussion addresses the question of 'Who is the greatest . . .?' — 'Who is the greatest soprano of them all?', 'Who is the best jazz artist?', and many more.

Since the music library was renamed the Rory Gallagher Music Library in 2004, it is now a place where his fans reminisce, share memories and feel close to 'the greatest guitarist of them all', so that it often seems as if Rory is not 'A Million Miles Away'.

Mary FitzGerald

Arched passageway to Rory Gallagher Music Library

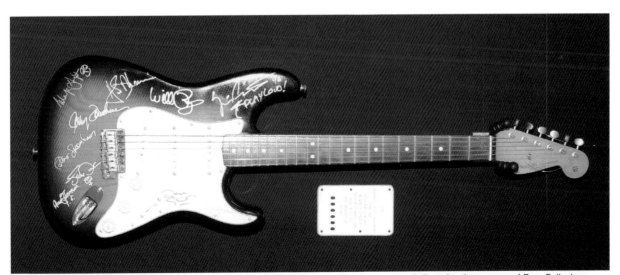

Fender Stratocaster guitar signed by participating musicians at 50th anniversary Wembley concert dedicated to the memory of Rory Gallagher.
Rory's brother Donal donated the guitar to Cork City Libraries at ceremony renaming the music department 'The Rory Gallagher Music Library' in
October 2004.

Uniquely, St Mary's Road Library

Our branch library, the oldest in service having opened in 1972, is snugly nestled between old Blackpool and the historic Shandon area. We also serve the bustling parishes of Gurranabraher and Farranree and outlying areas. In fact, we're right at the centre of things as Cork's northsiders funnel down through Shandon Street, North Main Street, and on into town.

St Mary's Road library is a quaint place, in its distinctive way: it's a place apart, warm and cosy, a welcoming, quiet haven amid the swirl of modern life, yet a maelstrom of activity when children from the four neighbouring schools invade us. Many libraries can make such claims and many offer broader services or spew out bigger statistics but St Mary's Road remains quite unique. We're like the butcher or the baker, the chemist, the convenient corner shop or the little local locksmith: we've been absorbed by the

Chess tournament in St Mary's Road Library

community — we are part of what they are. It's mainly first names here. They call us Ann, Clare, Chris, Eleanor or Gerry and we call them Martin, Tony, Mary, Bill, Tommy or Finbarr. It's just that kind of place, the Mr or Mrs bit doesn't last very long.

It's friendly in our library; friendliness is the essence of the place. Men from Blackpool, still a village in their minds, read the papers and spin us yarns about John 'Kid' Cronin or Jack Lynch or Mossie Keane. They often strike up conversations among themselves in the local patois about the harriers, or road bowling — particular passions up here; it's usually loud and fairly colourful! This place has character and characters. We get through a lot of yarns together. We hear their problems too, offering an unofficial confessional and counselling service – whether we want to or not! Northsiders are persuasive like that.

Other people drop in to us now, more and more. In the media, these people are called 'non-Irish nationals' and there is a large community of them in the area. We know them as Mehdi and Ngoie and Dusan, to name a few. We've watched them arrive from deepest Africa or the heart of Eastern Europe, often with poor English, and we've seen them stay here, learn more, get jobs, get somewhere proper to live, start following Cork City FC, become Leesiders-elect. Sometimes they tell us about their own lives. Some of the stories I've heard are harrowing.

There was one from a Somali that I'll never forget. But it's great to be a part of that, to actually help people get on with their lives. This place, I often think, is their first foothold in Cork, their first step to surviving in Ireland.

Being near the North Chapel, we're used to having tourists pop in for five minutes looking for directions to Patrick Street or St Finbarre's Cathedral, or, worst of all, to find their ancestors — "Like, they're over there in the Homer Bar!" as one of our regulars quipped once when a particularly overbearing American had just left, hot on the trail of his forebears. Now, though, they also call in to use the Internet to keep up to speed or let the folks back home know how they are getting on. For a lot of people now, our library is like a substitute office; they'll use the computers, e-mail, do up their CVs, check stuff in the reference section or just do some recreational surfing.

We've all the normal library services here, but we also occasionally mind the shopping while a visit is paid to Hackett's next door to place a bet; or keep the swag of half a dozen large-print books while someone goes to the surgery across the way. We do plenty more besides, well beyond the job description, but it's just all in the way of being neighbourly!

Gerry Desmond

Tory Top Library

Tory Top Library is a unique name for a unique library, unique as those who use it. Situated on a corner at the top of Tory Top Road, this library is a place of social interaction and strong community spirit, where reading the daily newspapers can be humorously controversial. Often noisier than the children, retired men insist that the staff take sides in their debates.

Gone is the silence of the hallowed halls of yesterday's libraries, now replaced by shrieks of delight as children enjoy puppet-shows, plays, story-times and even live animal workshops.

Teenagers bustle at the Internet, alongside mothers anxious to make that online purchase or to contact family members abroad.
No two days are the same. This a library where children stand in awe as Santa arrives with presents in a taxi or when an Easter bunny arrives on the number 3 bus!

Many happy times were had in the old library, with Christmas concerts where young and old came together to party and sing, or with Bookclub discussions on Frank O'Connor, or dance workshops and even relaxation therapy.

Since the knocking of the 30-year-old building, expressions of concern about when we would be back were constant. Frequent greetings of "Miss ye", "Hope ye will be back soon", "What will we do without ye?" were encouraging and motivating.

The sincere and friendly people of Ballyphehane deserve the new state-of-the-art library now open. Its success may be judged by statistics of books issued, but it is the people and the sense of community that makes this library unique and such a pleasure to work in.

Breda Hassett, Patricia Looney, John O'Leary,
Eleanor Twomey, Eugene Mulcahy,
and Marie O'Callaghan — Tory Top Library Staff

Breda, Marie, and library users after opening of new Tory Top Library

Douglas Library:
At the heart of the community

Jointly funded by Cork City Council and Cork County Council, Douglas Library is situated next to the Post Office in a very busy shopping centre. As well as lending books and audio materials to more than 5,000 registered members, the library provides a wide range of services to the Douglas community and environs.

At 10.00 a.m. each morning, customers arrive to read the daily papers, do some photocopying, book a session on the Internet, scan and e-mail an important document, engage in research or study, return, renew & borrow books, and check the notice boards for what's on in the coming week. The library is also a popular spot for visitors looking for directions and for local tourist information.

School children from the nearby schools arrive in class groups to return books and excitedly choose different books. A quick play with the doll's house when the teacher isn't looking is also part of the visit before they are reluctantly herded back to school. Pre-schoolers practise their colouring skills, while mum has a welcome read of one of the popular magazines in stock or a chat with another mum. "Have ye any cage?" was a desperate plea from a harassed granddad on one occasion! Dads are a common species on Saturday mornings, sometimes attracting a gathering of other little people while reading stories to their own child.

Various festivals throughout the year introduce children to different activities, including juggling, puppet shows, arts & crafts, and the occasional encounter with some exotic wildlife adds colour and excitement to the library experience.

Regular cultural activities take place for adults; these include the very popular Gramophone Circle mornings, when up to 50 people gather to listen to a pleasant hour of light classical music, and afterwards retire to one of the excellent hostelries in Douglas for lunch and conversation. The library plays host to two reading groups, one during the day and the Night Owls club which meets in the evening. Book clubs are a great way to broaden

Gramophone Circle meeting in Douglas Library

customer's reading repertoire and to make friends. The groups also organize literary trips to place of interest, and invite guest speakers to talk to them.

An bhfuil suim agat sa Ghaeilge? The Ciorcal Comhrá meets once a month to practice the cúpla focal, occasionally bursting into song and high spirits, earning quizzical looks from foreign visitors.

The library is frequently used by local groups to showcase their works. Exhibitions have included paintings,

photographs, craft work, wood, batik, quilts and many more. Lectures and talks are held on a regular basis, usually on Thursday or Friday evenings when the library is open until 8.30 p.m. We in Douglas Library are happy to be of assistance to our community and will continue to do our best to make your library a facility that is welcoming to all.

Peggy Barrett, Martin Byrne, Fionuala Ronan, Rebecca Crichton, and Sheila O'Sullivan — Douglas library staff

Mayfield Library / Leabharlann Bhaile na mBocht

The first thing that one notices when coming to live or work in Mayfield is the vibrant community spirit and the humour and warmth of its residents. Even though the area is quite large, everybody seems to know one another; all ages are involved in the many clubs, organisations, self-help groups and art societies, keeping alive that sense of community. This is very apparent on a visit to Mayfield Library. Whether one comes to relax and browse, to read a newspaper or magazine, or for a special event like a book-club meeting, a gramophone recital, a lecture, to look at an art exhibition, to partake in a storytelling session for children, or just for a chat, one will invariably meet someone they know or will meet a new friend. At times, the space can be a haven of tranquillity with just the gentle clickity-clack of computer keyboards; other times its as if bedlam descended on the place with what seems like thousands of children enjoying a puppet or magic show or in raptures listening to a favourite author visiting the library.

Let's not forget our local scholarly hero, Frank O'Connor, to whom the library is dedicated and to whom our permanent exhibition is dedicated; a literary giant whose short stories have been enjoyed by generations across the world. Let's not forget also Mayfield's other local hero, Roy Keane, whose many biographies grace library shelves and who inspires the local boys and girls, making a bee-line for the newest soccer books, whether it be on football technique or their favourite club. But the real heroes are the people of Mayfield who come rain, hail, or shine to visit their library to pluck the latest bestseller from the shelf, to acquaint us with the local gossip, or to just pass the time of day with us.

Sinéad Feely

Young users in Mayfield Library. Reading tree in background.

Hollyhill Library

The new branch library in Hollyhill opened its doors to the public on 6 January 1998. The library, which had been located in Terence MacSwiney Community College for many years, is now situated in the Hollyhill Shopping Centre. The change of premises had been planned for many years. By moving, the intention was to increase usage and membership of the library.

There is no doubt that the change in premises has given Hollyhill Library a new lease of life. Being in the Shopping Centre gives us a feeling of being part of the community. The library is more visible and more accessible. There is ample parking available, and the library is open during lunchtimes and also opens until 8.00 p.m. on Thursday nights.

Hollyhill Library is a modern, vibrant, state-of-the-art public library. The building is bright and welcoming, and houses an excellent bookstock for both children and adults. Over the years the non-book stock has been built up. There is now a wide range of audio tapes, video tapes, and more recently DVDs.

Currently there are eight Public PCs which are used by young and old. Internet usage is increasing all the time amongst adults and children. In particular there is a huge demand for the Driver Theory Test CDs, which can be used in the library by members and non-members alike.

Daily newspapers and a wide variety of magazines, for both adults and children, are available for reading on the premises. Our photocopying service is used frequently.

Hollyhill Library prides itself on being a positive asset to the community. The staff are known by first name to the customers. We have the time to get to know our customers' likes and dislikes.

We have a very high percentage of children using our library. As well as an excellent bookstock, children are spoilt for choice when it comes to activities. The traditional Saturday colouring competition takes place at 10.00 a.m. Between 9.30 a.m. and 10.00 a.m. the queue builds up outside the door and at 10.00 a.m. there is a rush of children in the door. Our day has well and truly begun! For our budding artists there is also a monthly colouring competition, which is done at home. Each week there are book quizzes to be completed and prizes to be won.

Every Saturday morning and Wednesday afternoon there is a meeting of the Chess Club. There is a growing interest in chess in Hollyhill. Our children have played in inter-library tournaments against children in the St Mary's Rd Library.

Our Gramophone Circle for adults is well established now. On the second Tuesday of every month we look forward to listening to the musical choices of the selected presenter. There is a pleasant, relaxing atmosphere in the library for the duration of each recital. During the year we also host talks for adults.

Art workshop in Hollyhill Library

Overall, we are delighted with our new location, and we will continue to strive to serve our community's needs.

Mary Corcoran

Readers Remember

Trips to the City Library were made not without a little fear and trepidation. The Children's library was guarded by the fiercest of all women. Hair pulled back into the most severe bun and dark clothes and round steel-framed granny glasses. We were convinced that she was placed on earth to scare the living daylights out of children and adults alike. Woe betide you if you incurred her not inconsiderable wrath.

Eddie O'Connell

It is unthinkable to contemplate life without libraries. Surely librarians are the most taken-for-granted people imaginable – always helpful, smiling and knowledgeable. Librarians should be collectively nominated for Cork Person of the Year. They are God's people.

Jim McKeon

Readers Remember

Laethanta geala ár n-óige
Do chabhraigh an Book Club go mór liom féin ar bhonn pearsanta, measaim,
níos mó ná aon ní eile. Bhíos cúthail an uair úd agus chabhraigh pé plé a
bhíodh idir chamáin ag an gcumann liom sa tslí is gur chuireas suim cheart
sna leabhair agus sa litríocht. Is dócha nár tháinig an bláthú déanach go
rabhas ag an dtríú leibhéal ach bhí an síol curtha. Chaith leabharlannaí na
bpáistí linn go fial flaithiúil, agus an rud ba thábhachtaí ná gur chaith sí linn
mar dhaoine fásta. Cuimhním go maith ar na turasanna go Baile Átha Cliath,
an turas go Londain agus an clár teilifíse a deineadh ar an gcumann.
Laethanta geala ár n-óige, gan aon agó.

Seán Ó Laoi

My best memory of the book club was making a short film which won top
prize at the international junior film festival. It felt like winning an
Oscar at the time. There were about 65 entries in total, so it was no mean
feat!

Cian Leahy

Gadaí i Leabharlann na Cathrach

Bhí sollúntacht éigin ag baint le Leabharlann na Cathrach, í neadaithe isteach go discréideach tromchúiseach i gcúinne Shráid an Chapaill Bhuí. Lean an mhistéir chéanna í is a lean séipéil Phrotastúnacha, nó Tithe Cúirte. Bhraiteas go rabhas ag siúl siar iseach i sean-newsreel de chuid an scannáin *Mise Éire* agus mé ag clárú inti an chéad lá, deasghnáth riachtanach eile mo theacht in inmhe fir, dar liom. Gnó an-fhásta suas feasta siúl isteach inti lem chárta ballraíochta chun leabhar a mhalartú. Eachtraí Adam McAdam, blianta luatha na meánscoile sa Mhon, is mó a fhanann im chuimhne. Céim eile in airde an Leabharlann Tagartha. Bhí tost níos tógálaí fós anseo, scoláirí fé ghloiní défhócasacha ag cogaint isteach go húdarásach in imleabhair mhóra stairiúla. *Elegy Written in a Country Churchyard* a bhí tar éis mo shuim i bhfilíocht mheadarachta an Bhéarla a mhúscailt i rang na Meánteiste agus bhí tógaint chroí ar leith ag baint le lámh a leagan ar chnuasach beag dánta ó aimsir na Romantics agus dul ag gadaíocht:

Bréagadh

A chailín gleoite de chuid North Pres.,
a bhí dhá bhliain romham
ag gabháil don Ardteist,
A shiúladh faram tráthnónaí boga fómhair
tar éis scoile síos Infirmary Road
i dtreo na cathrach,

na dánta úd a scríobhas duit
is a chuir oiread gliondair ort,
an bhfuilid fós agat?

Bhuel . . . níorbh ón láimh seo iad,
ach le mionfhile éigin gan ainm
in aimsir Wordsworth

a d'aimsíos i Leabharlann na Cathrach.
táim á adhmháil seo
tar éis dhá bhliain is daichead
toisc gur chuimhníos ort an lá cheana

is ar a tslí go gcuirteá
do mhéireanna im ghruaig

ag fiafraí an raibh
mo chuid 'curls real'
is go ndeargaínn.

Fén gcúigiú bliain bhí aithne curtha agam ar an mBuailtín agus ar Dhún Chaoin thiar, crú na teangan beo á dheargadh ionam agus rithimí mealltacha Eoghain Ruaidh Uí Shúilleabháin ag cursáil tríom. Bhí blaiseadh beag de Chúirt an Mheon Oíche curtha inár láthair ar scoil, cúpla sliocht neamhurchóideach nach raibh aon tagairt do rí-rá raibiléiseach na Cúirte féin iontu, gníomh cinsireachta, is dócha:

"Bhíodh éanlaith i gcrainn go meidhreach mómhar is léimneach
eilte i gcoillte im chóngar, géimhreach adhairce is radharc ar
shlóite tréanrith gadhar le Reynard rompu".

Bhí teist na conspóide agus na rúndachta ar an gCúirt. Caithfí dul á hiniúchadh. Agus b'in a dheineas, thar trí no ceithre bhabhta 'on the hop' ón scoil agus cúpla babhta tar éis scoile, i dtearmann na leabharlainne tagartha, an rud neamhcheadaithe ag cur breis priacail sa chúram agus breis faobhair ar mo ghoile:

"Siolladh dem shúil dár shamhlaíos uaim
do chonac mé chugham le ciumhais an chuain
an mhásach bholgach tholgach thaibhseach
chnámhach cholgach ghoirgeach ghaibhdeach".

Bhreachas síos na caisí aidiachtaí i leabhar nótaí, chuas á gcuardach i bhfoclóir an Duinnínigh, dheineas iontas dá líofacht is dá lúfaireacht shleamhain, mar a bheidís ina mbric in abhainn. D'fhilleadh 'an mhásach' arís orm roinnt mhaith blianta ina dhiaidh sin i ndán dár teideal Lúnasa. Tuilleadh gadaíochta!

Michael Davitt, 1950-2005

Michael Davitt, 1950-2005

What next?

Address: www.corkcitylibraries.ie/corkpastandpresent

Live Home Page   Apple   Apple Support   Apple Store   .Mac   Mac OS X   Microsoft MacTopia   Office for Macintosh   MSN

CORK CITY LIBRARIES ONLINE   **Leabharlanna Cathrach Chorcai**   Search the Site: enter query   go

LIBRARIES LEABHARLANNA

CORK CITY COUNCIL | COMHAIRLE CATHRACH CHORCAÍ

Cork Past & Present

| Home | About Us | History | Cork Images | Places |
| Cultural Events | Local Studies | Genealogy | Links | Contacts |

You are here: Home > Cultural Events

Cultural Events

Early History

Images & Text

Cork Places

St. Patrick's Street

What's On / Culture

The city's musical life is nourished by University College Cork, Department of Music and the Cork School of Music both of them important national centres of learning and research.

Cinema in Cork includes the Kino Cinema which offers a year-long programme of movies from around the world, and commercial cinemas such as the Gate Multiplex on Bachelor's Quay, the Capitol Cineplex on Grand Parade, Cinema World in Douglas, Cork Omniplex in Mahon Point, and the Reel Cinema in Blackpool. Information on current films is at http://www.entertainment.ie/.

Liam Ronayne

Cork's year as European Capital of Culture in 2005 offered enormous opportunities for the city's libraries to position themselves as centres of literature and culture, and the staff of the library were determined that these opportunities should be grasped. As the most visited public cultural space in the city, the Central Library hosted many events in 2005, including:

- Special exhibitions on Blues guitarist/songwriter Rory Gallagher; on the balladeers and songwriters of Cork; and on the city's classical music composers
- 'The Word Endures' seminar with an international panel of speakers, and an accompanying exhibition, both concerned with how libraries sustain freedom of expression
- An architectural ideas competition for a new Central Library design, run in conjunction with the Royal Institute of the Architects of Ireland
- High-profile 32-hour continuous opening of the Central Library for World Book Day readings and other cultural events
- A huge summer-long programme of events for children

S oon after Liam Ronayne was appointed City Librarian in April 2004, work began on the preparation of a five-year strategic plan for the period 2005-09. This plan, entitled Books, Bytes & Buildings, was adopted by Cork City Council in February 2005. It has often been remarked that strategic management is 10% planning and 90% implementation, and the implementation of the actions set out in the plan will involve every member of staff contributing their ideas and giving of their insights and special skills to ensure that Cork has the library service it needs in the twenty-first century.

Colm Tóibín reading
at Central Library
during Cork2005

For the staff of Cork City Libraries, 2005 offered enormous opportunities to position the libraries as centres of literature and culture, and to strengthen the library's role as a key strand in the city's cultural life. While 2005 is a landmark year for the city and for its library service, it is worth recording that the library has witnessed and served in other important years in the city's history; not only the celebrations for Cork 800 in 1985, but also the Cork Exhibition in 1902 and 1903 for example. The Libraries are an integral part of the permanent culture of the city; we were there before this signal year, and we will be there long after Cork 2005.

Cork 2005
European Capital of Culture

Children from Muine Fliuch National School, Macroom, advertising launch of City Libraries child summer-events brochure, 2005

Immigrants attending World Book Day readings on 23 April 2005

Denice McMahon and Jamie O'Connell visiting 'Chapter House' exhibit during Cork2005 European Capital of Culture special events in the Central Library

In addition to the cultural programme, progress has been made on providing new library facilities for the city:

- A new and larger Tory Top Library has been completed
- Work began in June 2005 on the construction of Bishopstown Library
- Initial planning is progressing for a library in the Blackrock–Mahon area.

As we saw in chapter 4, recent years have seen a major shift in how libraries are regarded and how the service perceives itself. Cork City Libraries are now concerned with the learning society, with social inclusion, and with a more participative cultural life, offering children the first and best chance to open doors to the world of knowledge.

For many decades the service was delivered only through the City Library in Grand Parade; from the early 1970s a number of branch libraries were opened. In the years and decades ahead the service will be delivered through three strands: (1) through the Central Library with its specialist services and the largest collections of stock for children and adults, a library with 4,700 square metres of public space is planned, more than three times what is available in the existing building; (2) through the network of local libraries serving all areas of the city with a range of services based on the real needs of the local communities being served; and (3) through an e-Library facility offering a full virtual library service with online transactions – registration, renewals, requests – and access to digital collections provided directly or via web links.

Cork City Libraries are ready to face the challenges of the future with renewed confidence, building on the accumulated knowledge and experience of generations of dedicated staff, and using all of the abilities of its current staff.

New Tory Top Library exterior

Internal garden of new Tory Top Library

Readers Remember

As the rain drenched Cork again, harassed damp people huddled in the doorway of the library for shelter. I edged in the soaked buggy. Once released, my little girl sprang into the brightly coloured room. "Library! Library! Sure I like the library, Mammy!" Her coat was pulled off and flung aside. Chubby fingers raked through the book box on the floor with the eagerness of a small digging animal. Treasures were celebrated with great exclamations. "I found Fairies, Mammy! I found Barney!" The small blonde whirlwind ran to the low shelves, where she picked up books at random, leafed through a page or two, before excitement took over and another one was grabbed. "Girl! Boy! Dog! Cat! Moon! Pink! Read this one for me, Mammy!" She straightened up to her full height of three foot and glared at me. "Now!"

We settled down to read. She acted out Snow White, slowly falling to the floor with one arm outstretched, then releasing the imaginary poisoned apple from small fingers.
We laughed at Little Miss Bossy and wondered at the magic of the Flower Fairies.
All too soon it was time to leave the library. The child moved off with a reluctant shuffle.
At the door, she looked up with bright hopeful eyes. "Sure we can go tomorrow, Mammy?"
I smiled and nodded gently. "Of course we can." Outside the rain had lightened to a damp drizzle, and my daughter filled up the air with songs all the way home.

Su Fagan

Readers Remember

I love the library and reading all kinds of books. A few years ago I had some oil paintings hung in Grand Parade Library, as a member of the Retired People's Network.

I felt very proud of that. My only regret is that I didn't learn to use a computer. I had my ninetieth birthday at the end of January (2005), so I am a long time on the road.

Joan Crowley

At your service...

Starting with just four staff in the 1890s, the complement of the Library has waxed and waned over the decades. There were 52 librarian/clerical staff employed in 1987, reflecting the expansion in library services in the 1970s and 1980s. This total included staff who administered library services in the Cork Regional Technical College (now the Cork Institute of Technology) and its constituent colleges (the School of Art, and the School of Music) for the City of Cork Vocational Educational Committee. In September 1987, however, staff numbers were dramatically reduced in line with the reduction of public service numbers nationally, and eight temporary staff were let go at one time. When the Regional Technical College / Cork Institute of Technology was constituted in December 1992, directly employing its own library staff, the staffing total in Cork City Libraries was reduced to 44. Numbers have increased in recent years and there are now 71 on the staff complement, including 14 part-time staff.

Until 1981 the staffing structure of the Library consisted of only three levels: Library Assistant, Assistant Librarian, and City Librarian. In 1981, the creation of two new grades, Senior Library Assistant and Executive Librarian, provided a more structured framework for the management and operation of the service; the three Executive Librarians have key responsibilities in running finance & staffing, purchasing and preparation of stock, and information & communications technologies, and the Senior Library Assistants help Assistant Librarians with administrative responsibilities.

Nine Assistant Librarians run the individual departments in Central Library and the five local libraries, while the Library Assistants, including part-time Library Assistants, are the public face of the service, the first and most important point of contact with users. Clerical staff play a vital role in support services for the Library, as do the attendant/cleaning staff throughout the six premises. The City Librarian has overall responsibility for the operation and development of the service.

The recruitment of 14 part-time Library Assistants in February 2003 enabled the Central Library to restore six-day service (Central had been closed on Mondays since summer 1987) and provide for lunchtime opening for the first time. This 38.5 per cent increase in Central opening hours, from 32.5 to 45 hours per week, is proving very popular with library users.

Writer Eoin Colfer, and his librarian character 'Spud Murphy' (third and second from right) on a visit to Cork City Libraries. Also in picture: Breda Hassett, Patricia Looney, Eileen O'Sullivan, Liam Ronayne (at back); Eleanor Twomey, Clare Doyle (in front).

IN SEPTEMBER 2005 THE STAFF COMPRISED:

City Librarian
Liam Ronayne

Executive Librarians
Anne Coleman
Eamonn Kirwan
Dr John Mullins

Assistant Librarians
Tina Healy
Kieran Burke
Kitty Buckley
Sinéad Feely
Peggy Barrett
Mary Corcoran
Mary FitzGerald
Breda Hassett
Patricia Looney
David O'Brien
Ann Riordan
Lucy Stewart

Senior Library Assistants
Martin Byrne
Bernard Cotter
Mary Coughlan
Deirbhile Dennehy

Gerry Desmond
Thomas McCarthy
(on secondment)
Helena O'Callaghan
John O'Leary
Tim O'Mahony
Sheila O'Mahony
Chérie O'Sullivan
Eileen O'Sullivan

Library Assistants
Alan Barrett
Catherine Creedon
Rebecca Crichton
Paul Devane
Clare Doyle
Matthew Farrell
Richard Feely
Dr Stephen Leach
Deirdre McAlister
Joye McKernan
Elizabeth McNamara
Claire Murphy
Laurence Murphy
Patrick O'Brien
Stephen O'Brien
Kate O'Callaghan

Mary O'Leary
Nigel O'Mahony
Paul O'Regan
Sheila O'Sullivan
Fionuala Ronan
Gerda Ryan
Eleanor Twomey

**Part-time
Library Assistants**
David Burke
Niall Connolly
Denise Hourihan
Elaine Howieson
Caroline Long-Nolan
Peggy McKenna
Denice McMahon
Elaine Moynihan
Marie O'Callaghan
Jamie O'Connell
Paula O'Keeffe
Leah Perez
Mary Sorensen
Joan Vaughan

Clerical Officers
Mary Twomey

Marion Haussmann (on leave)
Susie Maye
Nora Dineen
Mary Fox

Part-time Clerk
Aoife Rice

Porter
John O'Donovan

Cleaners
Betty McLean
Ann Lewsley
Peggy O'Connor
Marie O'Flynn
Claire McCarthy
Chris Smithers
Eleanor Flannery

Attendants
David Barrett
Harold Caulfield
Eugene Mulcahy
Michael O'Malley

Readers Remember

Some years after I married, the Douglas Branch was opened and my wife and I, both voracious readers, transferred our affections there. I cannot imagine a life without books and the many years of pleasure I have received through this branch of the library have been a great joy to me. I am eternally grateful to our City Fathers.
Ken Sheffield

I often wander to the Reference Library for information as well as treating myself to the monastic quiet that still obtains there. Long may we use the library, a treasure in our city. My first encounter with staff was due to our childish fear of all unknown adults. How could they have changed so magically in the intervening sixty years?
Mary Ahern

The decision to site a branch of Cork City Libraries in the Mayfield area has been vindicated as a wise and forward looking one from which many hundreds of local residents have benefited by having such a wonderful facility in our community. For my part, I have had the benefit of a high class library service that has been administered by a committed and dedicated staff to whom I am truly grateful.
Joseph Mullane

Readers Remember

The Library: A Personal Journey

9.55a.m. *I am waiting patiently at the door along with other early folk, a few "Good mornings", "Helloes", "How are things?", checking of watches, "The weather is bad", "Bertie is useless", "Charlie is worse", "Things are bad", and "The city is banjaxed".*

9.58a.m. *"Where is John?", "Is it the new fella!, watches checked, look in through the glass, "Tis 10!", "It's not!", "It is!", "OK so!".*

10.00.a.m. *"Ah! Here's John", (silent whisper) "About time!" Doors open, "Morning John", "Good man John, sound man", inside, dispersal of the troops, upstairs, straight ahead, left for papers, books to check-in, e-mails to be sent, notices to be read.*

10.01a.m. *Books checked in, quick march, past the rows of books, art, history, adventure, travel, cookery, D.I.Y, gardening. Fact and fiction, new books, old books. All waiting to be found and enjoyed.*

10.02a.m. *The music library is reached, good mornings and smiles all-round, straight to the racks of CDs, what new treasures await? Pop! Rock! Country! Jazz! Blues! Opera! Irish! World music! Classical! Soundtracks! Comedy! – with anticipation I begin my search.*

10.45a.m. *I approach the check-out desk, still reading the liner notes, I hand my membership card and CDs over to be checked out. "That's a great CD. Johnny Cash is brilliant! This got great reviews. Did you hear it on . . .?*
Thank you! See you next week! All the best!, good luck!"

10.47a.m. *Back to the books, that looks interesting, this looks like a good read, ok, I have what I want, checkout again, "Hi! I'll take these, thank you".*

11.00a.m. *Mission accomplished, through the barrier, CDs and books safely in the bag, walk through the city, can't wait to get home and already looking forward to next week's visit.*

Michael Cotter

Appendix I
Chronology of the Development of Cork City Libraries' Service Points

UNIT	DATE	SERVICE POINT
HEADQUARTERS	21 Dec. 1892 - 24 Jul. 1905 (Reading room); 1 Jul. 1893 – (Lending & Reference service)	Crawford Municipal Buildings, **EMMET PLACE** (Emmet Place was called Nelson Place until the early 1890s)
	12 Sep. 1905 - 11 Dec. 1920	Carnegie Library, **ANGLESEA STREET**
	12 Dec. 1920 - 28 Sep. '24 12 Dec. 1920 - 9 Jun. 1924	*No Lending library service* *No Reading-room service* (due to arson attack during War of Independence)
	29 Sep. 1924 - 17 May 1930 (Lending & Reference service); 10 Jun. 1924 - 17 May 1930 (Reading room)	**2 TUCKEY STREET** (In former R.I.C. barrack, now St V. de Paul premises)
	15 Sep. 1930 to date (Lending & Reference service); (Reading room since 21-5-1930)	**57-8 GRAND PARADE**
	22 Nov. 1976 to date	**57-61 GRAND PARADE** (incl. Music library since 10/7/1978 — moved to rear: 16/12/1983)
BRANCHES	12 Dec. 1972 to date	Branch Library, **ST MARY'S ROAD**
	16 Jul. 1974 to date	Branch Library, **TORY TOP ROAD** • In older premises until 10 Jan. 2004 • (Mobile service, Tory Top Park: 13 Feb. – 17 Dec. 04) • Reopened in new premises on 15 Sep. 2005
	17 Nov. 1976 to date	Branch Library, Village Shopping Centre, **DOUGLAS** • In two-storey units, nos. 30-31, until 1 Nov. 1991 • In ground-floor unit, no. 29, from 5 Nov. 1991
	17 Dec. 1980 to date	Branch Library, **HOLLYHILL** • in Community School until 20 Dec. 1997, and • in Units 7-8, Hollyhill Shopping Centre, since 6 Jan. 1998
	2 Nov. 1984 to date	Branch Library, Murmont, Old Youghal Rd, **MAYFIELD**
MOBILE	6 Oct. 1975 – 1 Apr. 1982	Mondays at Knockfree Avenue, **GURRANABRAHER**
	7 Oct. 1975 to date	Tuesday service at Curraheen Rd, **BISHOPSTOWN**
	8 Oct. 1975 – 1 Feb. 1984	Wednesday service behind Thomas Davis Street, off Glen Avenue, **BLACKPOOL**
	9 Oct. 1975 to date	Thursday service at **BLACKROCK** • at Skehard Rd until 18 Dec. 1997 • at The Pier, Blackrock Rd, since 8 Jan. 1998
	10 Oct. 1975 - 19 Oct. 1984	Fridays at Colmcille Avenue, Iona Park, **MAYFIELD**
	11 Oct. 1975 – 1 Feb. 1984	Saturday service at Ballinlough Rd, **BALLINLOUGH**

Appendix 2
Since 1892, the development of the City Libraries service has been under the stewardship of seven city librarians, in turn.

	City Librarian	Tenure
1	James Wilkinson	1892 – 1933
2	Eugene Carberry	1933 – 1955
3	Dermot Foley	1955 – 1960
4	James Gaffney	1961 – 1965
5	Seán Bohan	1965 – 1984
6	Hanna O'Sullivan	1986 – 2003
7	Liam Ronayne	2004 –

Appendix 3
First 100 years in figures

The two tables on the next page show one hundred year-end totals for items issued and for registered memberships in Cork City Libraries, since the establishment of circulation services in 1893. Figures for the six years 1993-8 were added in lieu of the missing records for years 1918-24. Table 1 shows annual totals for items issued or consulted during the same period. Table 2 shows the total of registered readers, but does not include the growing number of visiting readers who consult or browse newspapers, journals or books.

100 YEARS OF ANNUAL TOTALS OF ITEMS ISSUED BY CORK CITY LIBRARIES:

(Table 1) from commencement of issuing services on 1 July 1893 until 31 December 1998

(Items include books, journals, CDs, tapes, and Reference items, e.g., newspapers, microfilms, and maps)

Date	Issues	Library Milestones	Date	Issues	Library Milestones
1893	51,270	Emmet Place Lendg & Ref. from 1/7/1893	1946/7	277,651	
1894	92,670		1947/8	276,692	
1895	77,362		1948/9	278,615	
1896	78,735		1949/50	256,662	
1897	82,883		1950/1	222,928	
1898	87,447		1951/2	279,395	
1899	86,490		1952/3	284,448	
1900	90,731		1953/4	269,420	
1901	93,779		1954/5	274,556	
1902	94,440		1955/6	295,261	
1903	101,707		1956/7	321,937	
1904	101,859	Emmet Pl. library closed at end of 24/7/1905	1957/8	351,666	
1905/6	108,276	Library in Anglesea Street from 13/9/1905	1958/9	370,824	
1906/7	111,256		1959/60	390,561	
1907/8	98,483		1960/1	395,664	
1908/9	94,749		1961/2	411,596	
1909/10	94,041		1962/3	422,887	
1910/11	98,158		1963/4	378,905	
1911/12	100,090		1964/5	348,305	
1912/13	95,777		1965/6	440,055	
1913/14	94,017		1966/7	593,177	
1914/15	85,302		1967/8	605,193	
1915/16	84,148		1968/9	640,592	
1916/17	94,351		1969/70	616,303	
1917/18	101,912		1970/1	622,554	
1918/19	(no surviving		1971	606,159	
1919/20	records)		1972	608,016	St Mary's Rd branch opened: 12/12/72
1920/1		No Library service from end of 11/12/1920	1973	676,797	
1921/2	—	(No service	1974	732,640	Tory Top branch opened: 16/7/1974
1922/3	—	due to	1975	857,576	Mobile library opened: 6/10/1975
1923/4	—	fire damage)	1976	990,618	Douglas branch opened: 17/11/1976
1924/5	76,579	Lendg & Ref. in Tuckey Street from 29/9/24	1977	1,094,175	GP extension to departments completed in 1978
1925/6	117,927		1978	1,082,203	Music library opened: 10/7/1978
1926/7	120,469		1979	1,061,093	
1927/8	114,829		1980	1,079,767	Hollyhill branch opened: 17/12/1980
1928/9	121,328		1981	1,219,940	
1929/30	120,119	Tuckey St. library closed end of 17/5/1930	1982	1,147,808	Mobile ceased Gurranabraher service: 1/4/82
1930/1	125,517	Grand Parade Lendg & Ref. from 15/9/1930	1983	1,102,508	Mobile reduced to two-day service in Oct. 84
1931/2	182,231		1984	1,036,221	Mayfield branch opened: 2/11/1984
1932/3	213,694		1985	1,094,356	
1933/4	250,609		1986	1,057,976	
1934/5	331,054		1987	992,081	
1935/6	314,831		1988	959,106	
1936/7	283,736		1989	927,284	
1937/8	290,307		1990	906,079	
1938/9	300,009		1991	896,850	
1939/40	325,736		1992	910,401	
1940/1	390,120		1993	877,176	
1941/2	448,124		1994	800,635	
1942/3	448,870		1995	743,148	
1943/4	458,385		1996	780,507	
1944/5	405,612		1997	762,103	First Hollyhill branch closed at end of 20/12/1997
1945/6	332,427		1998	761,639	New Hollyhill branch opened: 6/1/98

* Music and Children's issues included. Reading Room statistics, opened on 22 December 1892, are not included.
Totals of Visits and Information Enquiries were not recorded for the above dates. *An audit year, e.g., 1953/4, which does not coincide with a calendar year, is dated from 1 April until 31 March*. Compiled from surviving annual reports (1892-3 to 1959/60) and in-house records of Cork City Libraries

100 YEARS OF ANNUAL TOTALS OF REGISTERED MEMBERS OF CORK CITY LIBRARIES

(Table 2) from commencement of Lending services on 1 July 1893 until 31 December 1998

Registered Music-library borrowers are included. Unregistered browsers, and Reference Library enquirers are not included.

Date	Borrowers	Library Milestones	Date	Borrowers	Library milestones
1893	3,131	Emmet Place Lendg & Ref. from 1/7/1893	1946/7	6,589	
1894	2,368		1947/8	7,070	
1895	2,171		1948/9	6,686	
1896	2,106		1949/50	6,820	
1897	2,294		1950/1	7,243	
1898	2,390		1951/2	7,305	
1899	2,209		1952/3	7,336	
1900	2,407		1953/4	7,421	
1901	2,375		1954/5	7,391	
1902	2,512		1955/6	8,545	
1903	2,532		1956/7	9,224	
1904	2,468	Emmet Place library closed end of 24/7/1905	1957/8	9,102	
1905/6	3,887	Library in Anglesea Street from 13/9/1905	1958/9	9,967	
1906/7	3,051		1959/60	10,787	
1907/8	2,606		1960/1	12,335	
1908/9	2,574		1961/2	13,217	
1909/10	2,449		1962/3	13,430	
1910/11	2,612		1963/4	11,308	
1911/12	2,659		1964/5	11,993	
1912/13	2,456		1965/6	18,219	
1913/14	2,443		1966/7	16,702	
1914/15	2,242		1967/8	15,985	
1915/16	2,394		1968/9	17,712	
1916/17	2,469		1969/70	17,071	
1917/18	2,769		1970/1	17,185	
1918/19	(no surviving		1971	17,355	
1919/20	records)		1972	18,634	St Mary's Rd branch opened: 12/12/72
1920/1		No service from end of 11/12/1920	1973	19,808	
1921/2	—	(No service	1974	21,976	Ballyphehane branch opened: 16/7/1974
1922/3	—	due to	1975	24,014	Mobile library opened: 6/10/1975
1923/4	—	fire damage)	1976	27,644	Douglas branch opened: 17/11/1976
1924/5	3,843	Lendg & Ref. in Tuckey Street: 29/9/1924	1977	27,288	GP extension to departments completed in 1978
1925/6	2,923		1978	24,682	Music library opened: 10/7/1978
1926/7	3,082		1979	25,455	
1927/8	2,818		1980	26,350	Hollyhill branch opened: 17/12/1980
1928/9	3,057		1981	30,093	
1929/30	3,078	Tuckey St. library closed at end of 17/5/1930	1982	28,965	Mobile ceased Gurranabraher service: 1/4/82
1930/1	4,478	Grand Parade Lendg & Ref. from 15/9/1930	1983	27,551	Mobile reduced to two-day weekly service Oct. 84
1931/2	4,447		1984	27,183	Mayfield branch opened: 2/11/1984
1932/3	5,694		1985	27,106	
1933/4	6,505		1986	24,611	
1934/5	7,319		1987	23,247	
1935/6	6,603		1988	21,994	
1936/7	5,894		1989	22,949	
1937/8	6,204		1990	23,128	
1938/9	6,534		1991	23,799	
1939/40	7,420		1992	25,218	
1940/1	8,550		1993	23,871	
1941/2	9,405		1994	21,563	
1942/3	9,555		1995	21,032	
1943/4	9,927		1996	22,981	
1944/5	8,824		1997	23,125	First Hollyhill branch closed at end of 20/12/1997
1945/6	6,732		1998	25,348	New Hollyhill branch opened: 6/1/98

An audit year, e.g., 1953/4, which does not coincide with a calendar year, is dated from 1 April until 31 March.
Compiled from surviving annual reports (1892-3 to 1959/60) and in-house records of Cork City Libraries

Select bibliography

Casteleyn, Mary. *A History of literacy and libraries in Ireland: the long traced pedigree.* Aldershot: Gower, 1984.

Cork City Council. *Books, bytes & buildings: Cork City Libraries strategic plan / Plean straitéiseach Leabharlanna Cathrach Chorcaí: 2005-2009*, ed. Liam Ronayne. [Bilingual parallel text.] Cork: Cork City Council, 2005.

Cork City Library. *First annual report of the Committee of the Cork (Free) Public Library to the Corporation of the city: 1892-3.* Cork: Guy, for Cork Corporation, 1894.

Cork City Library. [Annual reports of Cork City Library from 1892-3 to 1959/60] [varying titles]. Cork: Cork Corporation / Cork City Library, 1894-1961.

Cork Library Society. *Catalogue of books in the Cork Library Society.* Cork: Cork Library Society, 1808.

Department of the Environment. *Better local government: a programme for change.* Dublin: Stationery Office, 1996.

Department of the Environment and Local Government. *Branching out: a new public library service.* Chair: Tom O'Mahony. Dublin: Stationery Office, 1998.

Gardner, Frank M. *Public library legislation: a comparative study.* Paris: Unesco, 1971.

Great Britain. *Parliamentary Papers: Report from the select committee on public libraries together with the proceedings of the committee, minutes of evidence, and appendix*, HC 23 July 1849.

Grimes, Brendan. *Irish Carnegie libraries: a catalogue and architectural history.* Dublin: Irish Academic Press, 1998.

Irish Labour Party & Trade Union Congress. *Who burnt Cork city?: a tale of arson, loot, and murder: the evidence of over seventy witnesses.* Dublin: Irish Labour Party & Trade Union Congress, 1921.

Kennedy, Máire. "The Cork Library Society of 1801", *Journal of the Cork Historical and Archaeological Society*, vol. 94, 1989, pp. 56-73.

McCarthy, J. P. "Journeying to a journal: the Society's predecessors", *Journal of the Cork Historical and Archaeological Society*, vol. 96, 1991, pp. 1-18.

McCarthy, J. P. "In search of Cork's collecting traditions: from Kilcrea's library to the Boole Library of today", *Journal of the Cork Historical and Archaeological Society*, vol. 100, 1995, pp. 29-46.

Moody, T. W. *Thomas Davis: 1814-45.* Dublin: Hodges Figgis, 1945.

Mullins, John. Strategic learning and the challenges of change in Cork City Library: a case-study analysis of the development of information technology services. MComm thesis, National University of Ireland, Cork: 1999.

Neylon, Maura, & Henchy, Monica. *Public libraries in Ireland.* Dublin: University College Dublin: 1966.

O'Sullivan, Sylvester. "Andrew Carnegie and the reading public of Cork", *Evening Echo*, 7 January 1976, p. 5; "Cork's beautiful Carnegie Library had a short life", *Evening Echo*, 14 January 1976, p. 7.

Join a library, any library,
and the world becomes your oyster.

Noel O'Shaughnessy